RAF & RAJ

An Aircraftman's Life

1944 - 1948

To Les

With Best Wishes,

Jack Loveday

RAF & RAJ

An Aircraftman's Life

1944 - 1948

by

JACK LOVEDAY

Published by
J Loveday

Thorpe St. Andrew
NORWICH
Norfolk

© **Jack Loveday 2002**

ISBN 0-9544004-0-2

Illustrations by
Anita Loveday

Printed & Designed in England by
Barnwell's Print Ltd, Barnwell's Printing Works
Penfold Street, Aylsham, Norfolk, NR11 6ET
Telephone: +44 (0)1263 732767

INTRODUCTION

This account of my RAF Service tells no story of personal military bravery; indeed the reverse is usually true. Neither does it add overmuch to the broad sweep of RAF history. But it does record the trivia of daily life, the social history so often unrecorded or in some cases, such as the RAF India Mutiny, ignored by neglect or design. The book tells of my experiences at eighteen and during the three formative years that followed. Above all, it tells how I felt and how I reacted to people and events.

That it could be written at all is due to the fact that my mother kept all my letters - around 250 of them! Then there were diaries and ephemera to reinforce my memory of distant years. Most of the four years remain crystal clear.

Interesting places were seen and life was enriched by the comradeship of some wonderful people. The experience widened my horizons and acted as a kind of university of life.

In the book an attempt has been made to give an ordinary aircraftman's view of service life set against the background of world events. Historically it was a fascinating period. In 1944 the RAF was a powerful military machine with a vast personnel of one million. By the time I left it was a mere shadow of its former might.

It was the twilight period of the British Empire, the end of the Raj in India. For the British people exhausted by a long, cruel war, it was a time of great privation. All too soon we were overshadowed by a probable war against the USSR. Yet it was a time when many great reforms were carried out in the UK and servicemen returned to civilian life with hope for the future.

ACKNOWLEDGEMENTS

I am grateful to the following who gave me such invaluable help:
Merv Hambling, author of "Norfolk Crash Diaries".
Raymond Baxter, Broadcaster and Former Spitfire Pilot.
Alan Mallett with his formidable knowledge of merchant ships.
Superior Annie John of the St Thomas Mount Convent.
D T Barriskill of the Guildhall Library.
Peter Walker, author of "Norfolk Military Airfields".
Peter Sharpe who wrote "U-Boat Fact File".
Jak P Mallmann Showell, writer and authority on U-Boats, for information and photographs of U218.
Peter Turner, curator of the Manston and Spitfire Memorial Building.
Dick Ogden former Archives Manager of the Met Office.
The Community Relations Officer, RAF Coltishall.
Charles Farrow, local researcher for delving into RAF records on my behalf at the PRO, Kew.
The people of Skegness who responded to my appeal in their local newspapers for information.
Margaret Brown of Riverside Duplicating, Norwich for many hours of typing out my handwritten manuscript and for helpful advice.
Above all, my supportive family, for all their encouragement of my efforts.

CONTENTS

CHAPTER 1

On Becoming an 'Erk'

At the age of seventeen, already a member of the Air Training Corps, I volunteered for the RAF. This was no act of patriotism. As a cadet I was unlikely to be put in the Army or Royal Navy, but my ploy was to make doubly certain. The RAF, however, turned me down and suggested waiting for my call-up at eighteen.

Whilst in the ATC I had been seen by a selection officer in one of the Cambridge colleges. Some of my fellow interviewees told me they were volunteering for aircrew duties. When my turn came the officer seized upon the fact that I had school certificate maths, geography etc. and suggested I go before an Aircrew Selection Board. If successful I could train as a PNB (pilot/navigator/bomb aimer). At the time it was usually assumed that ex-grammar school boys interested in the RAF would wish to fly. This was encouraged by some ATC officers, themselves civilians and too old to fly, assuming they would have risked their own necks anyway.

When a look of reluctance showed on my face the selection officer put forward the suggestion that I would really like to, but was worried that I might upset my mother. I declined his offer pointing out my lack of any desire to fly. Wartime Norfolk had many aerodromes and we knew all about crashed aircraft. We cycled to crash sites, boys came to school with accounts of trapped young men in burning aeroplanes, usually bombers. It wasn't for me. I preferred being a live coward to a dead hero, but kept those thoughts to myself and the officer put me down as a flight-mechanic, maintaining aircraft, of which more later. Actually had I done aircrew training the war would probably have been over by the time I was operational, assuming I reached that far. Many trainees were killed in crashes. I have always had a deep admiration for those who did volunteer and usually paid the price, but it was not for me.

At this time I could have been drafted to a coalmine and not the RAF. Ten per cent of all 18-year-olds became Bevin Boys, as these press-ganged young miners were called. This lottery depended entirely upon the last digit of one's Identity Card number. This was done monthly. The first ballot was to take place on 14 December 1943. I would have been in the second one. Conscripts up to the age of 26 were affected. If you had the wrong ID card number you became a miner and were at greater risk than most RAF ground crews. The contribution of these young miners has gone largely unrecognised to this day, though at long last they were included in the Cenotaph March Past of November 1998 - long overdue.

Anyway, I escaped being a miner and eight weeks after my eighteenth birthday received, with mixed feelings, my call-up papers to report to RAF Cardington on 23 March 1944. On the day, I took a train from my home village, Melton Constable in Norfolk, travelling in the company of another recruit from Holt. On arrival at Bedford Railway Station we were joined by several others. We were then taken by RAF lorry to Cardington, at that time a vast reception centre. This RAF unit, as well as masses of huts for the housing of we 'sprogs' (recruits), had an enormous airship shed 274 metres x 56 metres. This had once housed the ill-fated R101 which crashed in France on 5 October 1930, one of my earliest recollections of an international event. The 'Daily Herald' at the time had photographs of a mass of tangled wreckage.

One of the first occurrences at the camp was the appearance of medical staff to check that we were free of venereal disease. This meant a mass dropping of trousers for an inspection known as an FFI (free from infection). After this, modesty no longer existed!

The Cardington experience lasted one week during which we received kit, were allocated trades and underwent all the necessary documentation. Each of us received a service number, mine being 3009731. The seven figure number beginning with 3 indicated an ex-ATC cadet. Non-ATC had numbers of seven figures beginning with 2.

My 3009731 had to be stamped on knife, fork and spoon, stencilled on the kit bag and printed in Indian ink on all clothing. The 731, known as the last three, became an essential part of my new identity as 731 AC2 Loveday. One's service number is indelibly stamped on the mind of every ex-serviceman or woman.

For better of worse, I was now well and truly an 'erk', said to have been a shortened form of 'air mechanic'. In the RAF an 'erk' was supposedly the lowest form of animal life.

One day we had identity photos taken. At this stage we still had only civilian clothing so we had to borrow ill-fitting tunics for the occasion. The order was to hold a board, on which had been chalked our service number, to look at the camera, and, above all, not to smile! We looked, and felt, like convicts and saw no reason to look happy anyway.

Two identity discs were issued, one red and one green. Each bore service number and name as well as religion - C. of E. in my case. The discs were made to withstand fire, blast or anything the enemy could throw at us. In the event of one's untimely death the body could be identified and given burial by the appropriate padre. The IDs had to be worn 'at all times' around the neck, secured by a piece of string. To be caught without 'dog tags' was an offence.

Some thought was given to allocating us an appropriate trade. The flight-mechanic idea was mercifully kicked into touch. I was, and remain, a mechanical moron and the astute interviewing officer recognised the fact. Had I been let loose on the air-frames or aero-engines of RAF aircraft this would have been a disaster. Court-martialled as a saboteur?

Seeing that I was keen on geography and reasonably proficient in maths I had suggested cartographical draughtsman, but no vacancies existed. At this time there was a need for more radar-wireless mechanics and meteorological assistants. The officer suggested the latter, which did really appeal to me.

Eventually we all donned uniforms and began to feel less like civilians. At this time each of our huts was a designated part of the Kitting Section, not a military-sounding title. One of the lads received a letter from his mother addressed to the Knitting Section.

One evening we were entertained by Joe Loss and his band, one of the famous 'Big Bands' of that era. The audience enjoyed it, repeatedly calling for, and eventually receiving, the band's theme tune 'In the Mood'. Whilst at Cardington we were also entertained by one of the RAF Gang Shows; great artists.

The evening before we left Cardington for Skegness, a veteran corporal of massively lengthy RAF service called into the billet to give his final words of advice. We had each been given a vintage Lee-Enfield rifle so the corporal's words were:

> *'Keep your rifles clean, shoot straight and honour the King'* - the *honour being pronounced with a sounded 'h'.*

With these fine words ringing in our ears we packed our pristine kitbags ready to travel on 30 March to Skegness to begin our 'square-bashing'.

This was an appalling time for the RAF. On the night 30/31 March as the result of a disastrous raid on Nuremberg, Bomber Command lost 95 aircraft. This represented almost ten per cent of the Command's heavy bomber strength. What impact would this have had upon we recruits? We had no access to a wireless-set (radio) and probably most of us did not buy a daily newspaper so immersed were we in what lay ahead at Skegness, so the event could even have passed virtually unnoticed at the time. But it is an appalling fact that during my first RAF week we had lost 180 bombers with an average of seven young men in each.

CHAPTER 2
Square-Bashing At Skeggie

RAF Skegness was the home of No. 11 Recruit Training Centre. This had opened in February 1941 and by the time it closed in October 1944 at least 80,000 young airmen had done their initial training at Skegness. Others were trained at places such as Padgate.

I was assigned to 3 Squad, 14 Flight, 2 Wing. There were thirty men in each squad, with four squads to a flight. Whilst I was there the unit strength would have varied from around 2,400 to 4,000. Certainly on Good Friday 1944 1,300 RAF personnel paraded for an open-air service, probably all of 2 Wing. There would also have existed two other wings.

The buildings used by the RAF were not of course purpose-built as on an aerodrome. Presumably the various hotels and houses in use had been commandeered by the Air Ministry. The Station Sick Quarters was the former Seacroft Special School on the Seacroft Esplanade. It is now the Seacroft Court Residential Home. The present-day Seacroft Hotel on Drummond Road was I believe Station Headquarters.

Our Airmen's Mess or 'cookhouse' as we knew it, was in the Grosvenor Hotel and the adjoining Imperial Hotel. This was situated on the North Parade/Scarbrough Avenue Corner.

The author at No. 11 Recruit Training Centre, Skegness. April 1944

I was billeted on the west side of Drummond Road in the company of several other squad members and a corporal. Here one slept, washed and spent what was left of the day cleaning equipment when drill, lectures and other RAF duties were ended. We managed to bath once a week, normally queuing for three-quarters of an hour at some kind of public bathhouse. This was always on a Sunday, the one day of the week when we had any free time.

Much of our training was spent on Tower Esplanade within sight of the Clock Tower. Here we marched under the watchful eyes of various NCOs (non-commissioned officers) - usually corporals who had a delightful vocabulary of abuse tinged with humour ('When I says eyes-front I wants to 'ear your eyeballs click'!). They attempted to convince us that we were the worst squad (until the next one!) that they had ever had the misfortune to encounter. On the Esplanade, now a car park, we were taught to perform numerous drills with a rifle to the cry of 'slope arms, order arms' etc. Sometimes we drilled with a fixed bayonet normally kept in a scabbard worn on the left side and attached to a harness of webbing. The whole thing had comparatively little military significance beyond the ceremonial aspect, but the main purpose would have been to make us instantly obey an order - in a sense to 'break' us. We were, however, not really bullied as has often happened to recruits in the services when harshness has crossed the borderline into the sadistic. For us much of the verbal abuse hurled at us was amusing and sometimes delivered with tongue in cheek. Our NCOs were decent types in the main.

The eight weeks training was closely identified with 'bullshit', 'bull' for short, that is 'spit and polish'. Boots had to shine with an unnatural brilliance achieved by wearisome hours spent boning with a knife, then endlessly polishing. Belt buckle, cap badge and buttons were all made of brass and had to be frequently polished and belts blancoed white. Hair had to be worn really short. I knew of this, so soon after arrival I had a short cut by a civilian hairdresser which I thought was a smart move. This still did not prevent being marched off with the rest to the RAF barber for an official shorning. For this tonsorial massacre we were 'advised' to give a threepenny tip. It was widely believed that our NCOs took a percentage of the gratuities we offered, which perhaps explained why we were such frequent visitors.

From the beginning it was apparent that an object to venerate was the rifle. We spent lots of time taking them to pieces. The barrels had to be cleaned by pulling through a piece of material known as a 'four by two' which was

14

attached to a length of string. Oiling was necessary and periodically a corporal would squint through to see that it was clean, sensibly oiled and contained no specks of dust. It was drummed into our heads that we should never point a weapon loaded or unloaded, towards anyone else, not even in fun. This we respected and is still sound advice. The previous year a Skegness recruit had accidentally shot one of his mates, fortunately not fatally. This had occurred in a billet on North Parade.

Somewhere along the front we did bayonet drill when we were encouraged to scream our abuse as we charged with fixed bayonets towards sacks stuffed with straw. Into the 'enemy', hanging from a wooden frame, we plunged our bayonets, removing same by placing a foot on the 'body'. Heaven knows how we could have done this in earnest, though a kill or be killed situation would have concentrated the mind somewhat.

There was also a session or two of unarmed combat. One instructor's face looked familiar. It was in fact Alf Young, who, pre-war, had played football for Huddersfield Town. He also played nine times for England between 1933 and 1939. Like many others the war ruined his career. For demonstration purposes we were convinced that the physical training instructors always chose the smaller recruits.

Skegness No. 2 Wing Airmen Mess 1942-1944, known at the time as the Imperial.

On 16 April, a Sunday, we had a military exercise the nature of which was never revealed to us. I remember being on my own lying with my rifle at the edge of a field. I ate my rations and endlessly waited for something to happen. Eventually I was told that I was no longer needed since I had been captured anyway. On examining the Operations Record Book 54 years later I found it had been a Station Defence exercise with full scale manning by all wings. Apart from minor details (was I one?) it had been deemed 'satisfactory'.

Initially firing practice was done with small bore .22 gauge rifles. This was quite good fun. Later, on 6 May, a wet, damp Saturday morning, we marched to Gibraltar Point to fire our personal .303 rifles. Targets had been placed in front of a sand dune. On revisiting the site for the first time in 1992 I found the sand dune overgrown with vegetation. Other banks of sand were forming on the seaward side.

We fired some normal rounds, then had to attempt to do the same by firing whilst wearing respirators. These tended to steam up. One poor lad who wore glasses had to take these off before putting on his respirator. With his limited vision he managed hits on a number of targets, with little in the way of bullet holes on his own!

I distinguished myself by some acceptable shooting, then must have become trigger-happy. Being keen to hit a target, a simulated man who would appear only briefly, I fired before the order was given and quite deservedly received a verbal lashing. I could have endangered the life of some unfortunate airman manipulating the targets.

Beyond the target area lay a stretch of sand, which, in 1944, was alongside the sea. Today the sea is much further out. At this spot each of us had to throw a live hand-grenade. Our orders were clear. Remove the pin, keep one's finger on the spring (there was no danger that I would do otherwise) then to throw the activated grenade from behind a sandbagged parapet in the general direction of the beach on the seaward side. We were then meant to count up to five, look to see where the grenade had landed, then, and only then, to duck behind the sandbags. Not being known for personal bravery I ducked immediately after throwing the grenade. This did not go down too well with our NCO. The latter I might add had the unenviable task of dealing with any dud unexploded missiles. Mine did at least go off!.

One day we fired sten guns, a cheaply produced weapon that could fire a single round or a short burst. The sten had an aperture at the side and, if held incorrectly, so we were warned, could take off the thumb and/or a fingertip - and no problem. I kept my fingers well out of harm's way.

I remember one incident when a recruit fired a burst of bullets instead of a single round, crying out as he did so: *'Corporal, I can't make it stop!'*

Fortunately he sprayed bullets towards the ground and not at, or through, his fellow airmen. I was not the perpetrator!

Once our feet in heavy boots had overcome the blistered stage, we were all really fit, strong enough to tackle the assault course. There, on a rough piece of ground where Castleton Boulevard met North Parade, we clambered over, through, and under, various obstacles. The area pre-war was known as the Jungle; now built upon it is the police station and courthouse.

We all had hearty appetites and looked forward eagerly to the cookhouse meals. The food was simple, but substantial and needed by teenage bodies being pushed harder in most cases than ever before, or in my case since. We queued outside the hotel and up a staircase to the first floor. The staircase, still there half a century later, had once had 'Died waiting' written on the wall, also 'Never have so many waited so long for so little'.

On one occasion we arrived at the Airmen's Mess tired and hungry only to be marched for some minor misdemeanour down Scarbrough Avenue. By the time we had marched back the long queue we had seen was even longer. The sergeant perpetrator of this piece of aggravation did nothing to enhance his popularity. Privileged NCOs never queued, simply walking past us to the head of the column.

Everything at Skegness had to conform to a set pattern with stacked blankets in line (no sheets). Spare kit had to be stored in one's kitbag and the slightest deviation in the routine could lead to a punishment. We each had our own knife, fork and spoon, known as 'irons' and a metal mess tin with folding handle. There was also an enamelled mug. At one inspection my mug was found wanting (slight tea stain) and I was required to scrub the cookhouse floor as a reminder of my iniquity - a large floor too!

On 8 May came respirator testing when we entered a gas chamber, later taking off our masks to experience tear gas. That evening we had a 2 Wing Concert. We clearly had some talented young men, including a superb ventriloquist. From 1,300 men there would have been a wide range of attainments covering music, art, sport and much else.

At this time an AC2 (Aircraftman 2nd Class) received a pay of twenty-one shillings a week (£1.05), but the RAF paid to the nearest five shillings (25p) so we received £2 each fortnight, the odd shillings being paid later. The pay was totally adequate for my needs being mainly spent on extra food and postage stamps. Foodwise the occasional parcel came from home, food they could ill-afford.

On the night 9/10 May two of us were detailed to guard a gun post where two Browning machine-guns were mounted at a point overlooking the Fairy Dell paddling pool.. The guard duty was a stretch from 20.00 hrs to 08.30 hrs. We alternated one hour on with one off. Standing there looking out towards the North Sea was the height of boredom. The theory behind it no doubt was that we were protecting one small segment of the English coast from the enemy - not that there was in the spring of 1944 the remotest chance of a German invasion.

After the guard duty, my 'finest hour' (England was safe that night!) we had a morning free to sleep, later in the day having our third set of inoculations. The first lot, soon after we had arrived at Skegness, caused sore arms sufficient for us to be excused rifle drill next day. It was amazing to see the deathly white faces of the airmen awaiting their 'jabs'. We even had the odd fainting case, yet a few years later I was to see tiny children face the prospect without batting an eyelid.

A week or so before the end of the course I narrowly escaped being put on a charge. Then, as now, the chewing of gum was common and on one occasion we were parading at our usual venue when a sergeant bellowed out that he could see an airman chewing. My immediate reaction was that some poor devil was in real trouble and that I would hate to be in his shoes (boots). Then, to my horror, the blood draining from my face and my throat going dry, I realised that I was the offending culprit. At the conclusion of the parade I presented myself, as ordered, to the sergeant and to my amazement received only a strong ticking off. He must have been in an affable mood, though he did not look it when offered my apology.

On 16 May I spent the day in the food stores and riding around in a lorry, dumping food at various cookhouses. Most of it was bread, margarine, meat and golden syrup in large 14lb (6.3kg) tins, four tins to a box - quite heavy I found.

Another duty during fatigue week was two or three nights of fire picket at the railway station. The various fatigues (duties) gave new experiences.

As well as doing so much square-bashing we had various lectures in the Arcadia Theatre. The site is now a car park. The instruction I enjoyed most was aircraft recognition which had been a hobby of mine since war broke out when I was thirteen. On one occasion we had a test when various photos and silhouettes were flashed onto a screen. I scored 47 out of 50 and such was my keenness that I was annoyed to have wrongly identified three. The importance of correct identification was all too evident. Many RAF 'planes flying in UK air space had been shot down by our own anti-aircraft guns, or, even worse in some ways, by one of our RAF aircraft. During the entire war I saw only one Luftwaffe aircraft, a Dornier 217 in 1943, yet I heard thousands flying over at night.

The above test had taken place on 17 May, the day we had a 3 Squad group photo taken in the Tower Gardens. From the photograph shine out the smiles of 29 young airmen, three corporals and an officer. I kept in contact with none. What happened to them, not only in the RAF, but also later? They came from a wide variety of occupations and social backgrounds. Did this really happen as long ago as 56 years?

Airmen of 3 Squad, 14 Flight, 2 Wing at RAF Skegness. Photo taken in the Tower Gardens on 17th May 1944. Author on left, second row from back.

The culmination of the initial training programme was the passing-out parade. The day before we had a full dress rehearsal watched by three or four squadron-leaders and two group-captains. They expressed their approval and general satisfaction with our preparedness.

The big parade was held on 23 May 1944 on the Tower Esplanade. The passing-out ceremony lasted only a few minutes. After eight weeks of coercion and cajoling we were declared as smart as Grenadier Guards. Looking back at what I wrote at the time I seem to have had a real sense of pride in what we had achieved. We must have looked good and certainly I was fitter than at any stage in my life. This was my physical peak.

Now we had passed out we had to make way for a new 14 Flight many of whom were young men from the Republic of Ireland (Eire), a neutral country. I am sure our NCOs were sorry to see us go since they now had to start all over again with raw recruits.

Our Drummond Road billet was needed for the newcomers and I was sent to a house on the North Parade, there to await my posting (transfer). It was to London. We all had to give our word of honour not to reveal our destinations and did so. Actually though I could see little military value in Hermann Goering's Luftwaffe knowing I was on my way to the plush St Regis Hotel in the West End's Cork Street.

Talking of the German Air Force I have no remembrance of the air raid sirens even sounding once whilst at Skegness. Earlier recruits had been less fortunate. During July to October 1942 fourteen members of the RAF had been killed in raids on Skegness with in addition around sixty injured.

Other dangers lurked. In 1942 an airman had been killed in a minefield accident; a WREN also died. Another young lady had been severely injured. I have no recollection of minefields.

On 27 May eight of us, including three from 14 Flight left by train for London to be trained as meteorological assistants. The remainder, most of whom had already gone, were sent to various RAF training units according to their various 'trades' as the RAF termed the different branches of the service. After trade training they would either stay in the UK or be dispersed to the various RAF aerodromes throughout the world.

CHAPTER 3
Met. Training In London

My posting from Skegness took me to Air Ministry Unit, RAF St Regis Hotel, Cork Street, London, W.1. What a posting it turned out to be. The St Regis accommodation and food, by RAF standards, were positively luxurious. The building was twelve storeys high and we were billeted only two or three men to a room. I shared with a lad named Dick Heard and we even had an en-suite bathroom. At the time I would not have described a bathroom as such. My only acquaintance with a bath was of the portable type that came in from an outhouse on a Friday evening, the water being heated in saucepans and kettles. Imagine using a bathroom for the first time at eighteen!

All airmen made food a major concern and here it was superb. I have fond memories of gorgeous trifles. Any that remained from dinner would be served for supper. Few attended the meal, but I made certain I was present for 'trifle suppers' - even second helpings were available.

At mealtimes an NCO would sometimes utter the magic words:

'Would you like any more, boys?'

Had we had enough? Here was an improvement on Skegness.

I even remember on arrival at the hotel being asked by a corporal whether he could carry my kitbag upstairs - unthinkable at Skegness. Three RAF units so far, but what a difference. This was how it was to be.

We had arrived on a Saturday and were given the following Monday off once we had had a kit inspection. This proved amusing. One of our number was a veteran of the Anzio landing in Italy when, from January to June 1944, a bridgehead was made behind the German lines. In the fighting this airman had lost much of his kit. Each time the inspecting corporal spotted items missing and queried same he received the stock reply:

'Well corporal I gave it away to a comrade in distress.'

This was said in such a droll voice. Beyond seething inwardly what could be said by the corporal?

That afternoon some of us were at Lords watching cricket, England v Australia. I well remember it being scorching hot, the match being well-attended, wartime or not. The cricket, however, remains a blank.

At Kilburn we were given instruction in all aspects of a met. assistant's work. The course was held in a vacated school. Each day we marched in shambling style from Cork Street to Piccadilly Circus taking a Bakerloo underground train to Kilburn Park. At Kilburn we were taught to identify cloud types and estimate their height. We familiarised ourselves with various pieces of met. equipment such as the thermometer, barometer, hygrometer and anemometer. This information, once we were on an aerodrome, would have to be passed to other aerodromes, usually in coded form. We in turn would receive other people's observations. The information received would have to be decoded, then plotted on synoptic charts using various symbols. All this information was bewildering, but had to be assimilated, partially at least, by the time the course finished.

Once on an aerodrome we would quite literally assist officers who did the actual weather forecasting. We would assemble the information. The forecasts, vital to aircrews, would never be done by us. The forecasters were either civilian Met Office personnel put into uniform, or 'called up' officers, including many ex-grammar school teachers.

RAF met. assistants at the training stage were AC2s. Once qualified, after working operationally on an aerodrome for a few months, we became AC1s, then LACs (leading aircraftmen). Some became corporals, a few sergeants. A minority only would become officers. I had no interest in the latter lacking the necessary self-confidence or social grace.

Our course trainees included fourteen soldiers from the Canadian Army, an RAF lad from Chile, the rest being British except for Pierre Eid. The latter was Belgian and I remember him for telling a fellow airman with some feeling:

'You are like zee pig in zee aquarium'.

Our rooms were inspected meticulously and as well as the obvious details such as a clean bath and wash-basin, an officer's finger would be run along the tops of doors seeking out specks of dust. Failing to pass room inspection meant deprivation of a 36 hour leave pass. These were only available to men living within 20 miles of the unit. For people outside this radius only a 24 hr pass was obtainable, no use to me for going home. This seemed a little absurd and the logic escaped me. The travel restriction was imposed to limit movement of personnel who had no urgent need to travel. Little did we know it, but tens of thousands of soldiers were being moved to the coast in preparation for D-Day and the landing in Normandy.

London was a strange city at this time. It was full of service types from so many different nations, though Britons and Americans were the most numerous; there seemed to be almost as many women as men. There were thousands of American officers, whilst as for our own RAF officers, they were more abundant than we humble AC2s. We were in such a minority that it was fully accepted that we did not salute each time we passed an officer. Our right arms would have ached had we done so.

For recreation there were recognised clubs for the various ranks and nationalities. One I frequently visited was mainly for Canadians and called the Beaver Club. Cinemas were open, but whereas in Skegness we paid 9d. (4p), in the West End seat prices ranged from four shillings and sixpence to 21 shillings (£1.05) - the latter being an AC2's pay for an entire week. There were also allocations of free tickets for live shows available to service personnel. Glenn Miller was in the London area though at the time I knew little of him. In retrospect I regret an opportunity lost.

On 6 June the long-awaited Second Front opened. In the early hours 176,000 men landed on the beaches of Normandy, a minority coming in by parachute or glider. The D-Day landing caused much excitement and we eagerly followed the unfolding of events in the daily newspapers or on the radio. The landing was successful, but had we attempted it in 1942 or 1943 as the Russians called for, it would have probably been a disaster.

CHAPTER 4
Hitler's Vengeance Weapon One

A week after D-Day on the night of 12/13 June, powerful and initially unexplained explosions took place in four different parts of London - some heard by us at the St Regis. From 16 June a succession of explosions occurred as Hitler's Vergeltungswaffe Eins (Vengeance Weapon One) fell on London and other areas of Southern England. These soon acquired the nicknames 'buzz bombs' or 'doodlebugs'. The Cabinet ruled that they must be known as flying bombs. The name of course mattered little to the poor devils on the receiving end. The era of warfare by remote control had been ushered in.

For a couple of weeks the V1s came over at the rate of around one hundred a day. The sound was unforgettable. They spluttered like enormous motor-bikes and when the motor cut they made a swift descent making a hellish roar as 850kg of explosives was detonated. The blast was enormous since there was so little ground penetration. A relatively small crater was produced compared to the conventional free-falling bomb. The characteristic V-1 sound was due to the fact that they were essentially jet-propelled and small explosions caused the rattling noise.

One day, standing outside the St Regis, some of us watched a Spitfire chasing a V-1. The V-1 with

Dick Heard with whom I shared a room at St. Regis.

a top speed of 400 mph (644 Km/h) looked faster. What the Spitfire pilot would have done had he caught it I have no idea. Over the sea or countryside V-1s were shot down, but not over built-up areas such as central London.

On Sunday 18 June occurred one of the worst incidents in the V-1 onslaught. A direct hit was scored on the Guards' Chapel, Wellington Barracks in Birdcage Walk. The 106-year old building collapsed killing 119 people and badly injuring 141 others. These were service personnel and civilians attending a morning service. The St Regis was only three-quarters of a mile from the Guards' Chapel and we also had a service in progress at the same time. Some time after 11.00 we heard a V-1 roaring in, then exploding almost immediately. It could so easily have been us. The service over I walked to the scene and picked up from the road a small piece of V-1 metal.

On 25 June I visited Regent's Park Zoo which had been bombed the previous week. Dozens of windows had been smashed, many roofs had been blown off, but the zoo was still open to the public. The poor tortoises were still covered in dust. For safety's sake some of the more dangerous animals had been destroyed earlier. There were giraffes, zebras and rhinoceroses, but no elephants. There was also a lion which had been presented by Winston Churchill.

The V-1s formed a background to our course work at the Kilburn School. We were at the top of the building in a room facing south which roughly was the direction from which the flying-bombs came. We watched them in fascinated horror mixed with excitement, in spite of one ultra-keen Scot who kept telling us to get on with our work which he managed to do, ignoring the V-1s completely.

One day, 28 June, from that window I watched two V-1s come down and explode, two others flying along without exploding and heard eight others hit the ground then explode in the distance. One V-1 I had watched for around twenty seconds before its engine stopped. It then plunged in an arc into the ground with a deafening roar, followed by a large column of black smoke, then 'woof' as the blast passed us. All I hoped was that we would never see one descending towards the school. The above took place in just a few hours in one area of London. My pal, Dick, who was a Londoner, said his mother had heard thirty one night.

The wretched things were a totally indiscriminate weapon liable to explode, at any time, anywhere. My attitude towards them as an 18-year-old can only be described as one of fascinated intense interest mingled with fear, aware that here was something new in warfare.

If one was in the flight path of an approaching V-1 there were two situations to hope for - either that it would fall short, or else fly well beyond. Curiously enough, once the missile was overhead there was a feeling of relative safety. If at that point the engine cut, then the curved path of descent would take the bomb well past oneself, or so I had concluded. Such is one's desire for personal survival that all that mattered was for the V-1 to fall elsewhere. Yet I had seen the devastation they caused. I have in mind a block of flats sliced open as if by a gigantic knife. This was near the Tottenham Court Road, recently hit with all the poor families' belongings in view.

All this air activity belied something I had written a few days earlier:

'Fewer V-1s, mainly at night or on cloudy days.'

On 29 June one exploded near Piccadilly, a quarter of a mile from the St Regis. Next day there was a horrendous incident at Aldwych. I heard that one approach as I walked through a West End street containing plate glass windows. There was usually a warning period of several seconds between the time the engine stopped and the moment of impact. It was normally possible to count from one to ten. As the 'Aldwych' V-1 approached I scampered in record time for the comparative safety of the entrance to an underground station. Before the 'ten' was reached I was safe, but not so around 25 people killed. Aldwych, it being 2 p.m., was crowded. It was this type of situation that caused the worst casualties.

On a Sunday morning, 2 July, I decided to take a walk to the Dockland area, badly hit by the 1940-1941 Luftwaffe attacks on the East End. I walked as far as Poplar by the West India Docks. It was interesting, but shocking to see the earlier destruction in this mainly poor area.

The walk became rather scary when, to my horror, I saw many V-1s approaching. To make it even more disconcerting was the knowledge that at this time some flew straight into the ground with engines still going. The arrival of V-1s was irregular - there could be a steady stream or a lull, but sometimes they left the launching-pads in batches. This depended on the weather and on the numbers shot down by anti-aircraft guns and the RAF, before reaching London. Anyway I felt too exposed to linger in open ground and hurried to the slighter safety of the streets.

In spite of the fact that most Met. Office personnel were in uniform it remained a civilian organisation. Coming from Norfolk which was sparsely populated, but yet was full of aerodromes, my chance of a Norfolk posting looked promising. Failing that, I hoped for somewhere in East Anglia, otherwise perhaps I could swap postings with someone.

On 28 June the postings came through and mine was to RAF Coltishall. I was delighted since this aerodrome was only eighteen miles from home. One other person had been posted there, this was John from the Wirral, a man whose education and culture were far superior to mine. It was John who took me to see my first D'Oyle Carte performance when we saw 'The Mikado'. Politically we did not always agree as I was well left of centre, but he helped me.

The posting, a good one, had a downside, not known at the time. After a few months in the UK most of us would be going to the Far East. Most met. assistants were WAAFs, who were not sent to South East Asia Command, so this was our destination.

The course was completed on 3 July and as far as I knew everyone passed. Next day we had a medical examination (again!) and on the 5th I was given a special assignment - report to the cookhouse and shell peas! The V-1s were still coming over and the air raid siren often sounded six or so times a day. Before the V-1 attack was over around 5,500 people had been killed, mainly civilians. When I left London on 6 July they were still coming over thick and fast.

London had been an interesting experience and I had met well-read, intelligent people from whom I had acquired fresh ideas and widened my horizons. One airman had left school to work in a slate quarry, studied in his spare-time and entered the University of Wales. He was a trade unionist and had been to Geneva to attend conferences. We spent hours talking politics. I cannot recall his name, but I am sure he made his mark in the political field.

My abiding memory of that segment of my RAF service is of the V-1s, a London swarming with officers and the comfortable St Regis Hotel. The V-1s left a brief legacy, namely, that on arrival at Coltishall, for the first few days I flinched on hearing an aircraft.

CHAPTER 5
A Fighter Station At War

The journey from London back to Norfolk is now almost a blank though I do recall the familiar accent as we stopped at each country station. There was a total black-out and anyway the station name signs had been well obliterated by black paint. Porters called out the names of the stations, unintelligible to some passengers, though not to me.

Eventually we arrived at Buxton from where RAF lorries took us to the aerodrome. Coltishall was an ADGB fighter station i.e. Air Defence of Great Britain. Here we were billeted in one of the solidly-built H-type barrack blocks, so named because of their shape. My room-mates were all on the Station Headquarters staff. The HQ staff consisted of men who were not members of squadrons. The latter moved fairly frequently. As the aircraft changed base so their ground staff (fitters, riggers etc.) moved with them, a few by air, most by other slower means. Their loyalty was to their squadron as infantryman's allegiance was to their regiment. But HQ staff were in a sense working for the aerodrome. Each RAF Station was self-contained with its own cooks, drivers, medical officers, nurses - even shoemakers.

The H-blocks were spartan, but warm and comfortable though there was precious little privacy. Each airman had a bed, blankets and a steel locker. They were superior to Nissen huts; good accommodation really.

Many of my fellow-residents were 'old sweats' who had been in the RAF many years. Amongst these men I was a new boy and felt acutely conscious of it. I felt like a child entering a new school, though settling in fairly quickly.

One privileged airman had pre-war been either a farm-worker or gardener living near the aerodrome. On call-up he was eventually posted to Coltishall where the RAF employed him as a gardener. I was told he had been there for most of the war, presumably often being at home. It was what the RAF called a 'cushy posting'.

As well as new living companions I also had to fit in with new workmates. Although theoretically a qualified met. assistant I had neither the practical experience nor yet the work speed to be of much use to the forecasters on my own. It was many weeks before I was capable of doing a solo duty and I worked under the supervision of a WAAF, someone highly skilled and with the job completely understood.

My mentor was an LAC named Betty Moore, a lovely person of 22, petite and attractive and certainly patient as a supervisor. Betty was a good hockey player who after the war toured Europe playing for a WAAF team and also played for England's second team.

Under her tuition I gained gradually a fair measure of competence. For estimating visibility we used various landmarks (church towers etc.) whose distances from us were accurately known. In misty conditions at night Flying-Control occasionally gave us permission to switch on the outer circle lights - quite a thrill to do in blacked out Britain!

To estimate cloud height we sometimes used, time permitting that is, hydrogen-filled balloons which ascended at a pre-determined rate per minute - providing we did not overfill or underfill the balloon. Temperatures, pressure, wind speed and direction, hours of sun each day - all had to be recorded.

The Met. Office had I think four officer forecasters, three airmen and several WAAFs. One of the latter was writing a book about an aeroplane. I wonder if her 'Tiffy the Typhoon' was ever published? Looking back they were a good crowd to have worked with and in this I was fortunate.

Via our teleprinter we received weather reports from RAF aerodromes and Atlantic weather ships. These reports were transmitted in five-figure groups according to an international meteorological code. This information had to be plotted onto large charts that showed the British Isles and parts of western Europe. The pens we used were of the old school type with a wooden handle and steel nib. Plots were done in red or black ink. To work at speed two pens were tied together, one for each colour. This antiquated method would seem almost Dickensian today, but it worked effectively. I enjoyed plotting these charts, but liked to complete the whole thing myself and hated finishing someone else's work.

Every hour we had to leave the inside work and do a weather observation - partly from the top of the Control Tower building and partly by reading the instruments kept outside in the Stevenson screen. The inside of our office was well illuminated and outside in the darkness a period of adjustment for the eyes was always needed before tackling the hourly 'ob'.

One day something from the teleprinter had me bewildered. Messages came through in a code I did not recognise. The officer in charge wrote down for my benefit a method of decoding, told me to commit it to memory, then produced a lighter and reduced the decoding paper to ashes. I was intrigued.

When I plotted the data I found the information concerned the weather over parts of Germany. Some thirty years after the war ended closely guarded secrets were revealed and for years I was convinced that I had been using information supplied by code-breakers at Bletchley. A more mundane explanation could be that the details of German weather were the work of an RAF Meteorological Flight Aircraft. These reports came in spasmodically in their double code. For 50 years the Bletchley code-breaking of German weather reports remained classified information. If I was not using Station 'X' information why all the secrecy? In time of war the individual sees only a minute part of the overall picture, as if one possessed a few pieces of a gigantic jig-saw puzzle of great complexity.

Our Met. Office was situated in the Control Tower building which gave us a unique opportunity to acquire all the latest 'gen' (information) on what was happening on the airfield. The duty Flying Control officer was responsible for all aircraft taking off or landing, or for any movement (human or animal) on his territory. The FCO usually passed news of interesting happenings to our own officers. With pilots often coming in for the latest weather 'gen' - or just for a chat - my ears were usually flapping. For an 18-year-old who had spent his teenage in a nation at war and who was interested in military aviation the large-windowed FC office was the place to be; Met. next door was the next best place on the whole aerodrome. Something of interest was invariably happening and I found it fascinating.

Not so fascinating was our teleprinter on which I could tap out figures with ease, but a mixture of words and figures to be transmitted had me floundering. A Mosquito crew gave us weather news which I had to send to Group HQ Watnall. My snail's pace prompted from the receiver, *'Come on Weary Willy!'*.

To return to the airfield. In one incident a USAAF B-24 landed in desperate plight making it to us with three minutes fuel left.

From 8 September 1944 onwards a new chapter in the world of military frightfulness appeared, the V-2 rocket, forerunner of all future rocketry, military or civil. It could not be intercepted and arrived swiftly and unexpectedly. In a built-up area it was devastating. In all, 1,115 landed on UK soil, London being the main aiming point, though Norwich too was targeted, though unsuccessfully.

From the top of our tower, if weather conditions were right, it was possible to see the upward moving 'Big Ben' condensation trails of V-2s being launched from the Netherlands. This was only a hundred or so miles from Coltishall and we were as near the launching pads as we were to London.

A post-war civilian pilot on the Norwich-Netherlands route once told me that on a clear night he was able to see the lights of Rotterdam and Amsterdam before crossing the Norfolk coastline.

CHAPTER 6
A Double Life

When I arrived at Coltishall there were three squadrons there. 25 Squadron was equipped with Mosquitos, Mark XVIIs which was a night version of this versatile aircraft. It was twin-engined and had a crew of two. This squadron often flew with the main RAF bomber stream heading for German targets. The idea was to shoot down any Luftwaffe night fighters intent on shooting down our Lancasters and Halifaxes. They also flew in the vicinity of the German aerodromes hoping to catch enemy fighters as they were about to land. Their squadron motto was rather apt - 'Striking I Defend'. The squadron stayed at Coltishall until 27 October 1944 when it was transferred to Castle Camps, Cambs. In nine months they destroyed 24 German 'planes and 22 V-1s.

There were also two Spitfire Squadrons. No 312 Squadron was a Czech unit formed in 1940. Unit motto: 'Not Many Men but Many Deeds'. They flew Spitfire 1Xs by day escorting American B-17s and B-24s as well as RAF bombers over enemy territory. Their stay at our base was brief (11 July - 27 August 1944) then they departed to North Weald, Essex which was a famous Battle of Britain aerodrome. 312 Squadron had been formed at Duxford another Battle of Britain station.

229 Squadron also flew Spitfire 1Xs doing the same bomber escort work as 312. Both squadrons did attacks on any shipping found hugging the Dutch coastline. Their motto was simple - 'Be Bold'. Staying with us from 1 July - 25 September 1944 they then moved to yet another Battle of Britain aerodrome, Manston in Kent.

Whether warplanes with their destructive capacity can be described as beautiful might be considered debatable. Certainly both the Spitfire (except for the clipped wing variant) and Mosquito were aerodynamically perfect. Both the 'Spit' and the 'Mossie' were streamlined, sleek and elegant from whatever angle you saw them fly. But on the ground a Spitfire pilot had a restricted field of vision. On taking off on our grass runways they veritably waddled and were not at all as attractive as in the air. But all those years later the sight and sound of a Spitfire causes the hairs at the back of my head to bristle. At the end of the war when most Spitfires were scrapped one could have been bought for £100 or so. What an investment! But who had the money? Or even the interest. People were sick of killing machines.

Of the Mosquito may I say one of our WAAFs was mad keen to fly in one, but none of the pilots could risk an unauthorised passenger even if the flight be for 'weather purposes'. No doubt in the Soviet Union this lass would have been flying a Stormovik.

On 6 October a Mosquito XII of the Polish 317 Squadron crashed. The Poles were based at Church Fenton, Yorks but had a detachment at Coltishall. This particular aircraft swung on take-off, not an uncommon occurrence, hit two parked Tempests, plus a lorry, ending up against a hangar wall. It narrowly missed the Control Tower and when I reported for duty, looking at the tyre marks of the Mosquito, I calculated the starboard (right) wing tip must have missed our building by only a few feet. My colleagues inside would have had real problems had the building been hit by an aircraft full of aviation fuel. As it was none of them made overmuch of the incident, but then our young ladies were quite unflappable.

In the office we worked to a duty roster, the periods being known as early (08.00 - 17.00), late (17.00 - 23.00) and night (23.00 - 08.00). For many weeks the sequence ran as follows - late, late, night, night, early, early, day off. Once the second early duty was over we had 48 hours of freedom. The problem however, was that we were officially allowed only 24 hours off camp, but I disappeared home for the full 48 hours running the risk of being caught.

I solved the pass problem by using an authentic one signed by one of our officers to cover the first 24 hours. For the second period I acquired a duplicate pass on which I forged the signature of the same officer and became quite skilled at this deception.

The one difficulty was that we were supposed to book in and out of the Station Guardroom manned by SPs (Station Police). This building I simply ignored and cycled straight past it. Outside the aerodrome perimeter was a road block manned by an SP corporal. One of his duties was to check passes. Having a telephone he could contact the Guardroom to see that we had actually booked out. They seldom bothered, but on one occasion the SP did ask if I had booked out. I bluffed my way out of it. The more I made my 'escape' the less it bothered me. It could have landed me in real trouble, but having conscientiously done my work it seemed silly not to take advantage of a 48 hour break.

For a teenager I was leading a strange double existence as on the occasion when a squadron of Spitfires was needed to attack V-2 sites in the Netherlands. Poor visibility made take-off conditions dodgy so the forecaster asked me to go on the roof and estimate the visibility. On my word alone twelve Spitfires flew off, quite a responsibility - and a thrill. Yet a short time later, duty completed, I could well have been cycling the few miles to the railway station at Felmingham. I used to put my bike in the guard's van and I was off.

At the end lay a different world - home comforts, the company of my parents and brother, my own bed after an evening by an open fire. Up early, then back once more to that other world consisting of barrack blocks, the Met. Office in the Control Tower, the NAAFI, Church Army canteen - and aeroplanes! What a characteristic smell when I passed a hangar or dispersal point. The Spitfires and Mosquitos being serviced gave off an aroma of hot metal, rubber, aviation fuel, oil and dope.

Cycling back to Coltishall on a clear night I could see the Sandra lights miles off. Three searchlights were directed upwards forming an overhead cone. They gave me a sense of nervous anticipation.

I was home at every opportunity once my duties were over, cycling the 18 miles if train times were inconvenient. Weather was no deterrence. Some evenings during the 44/45 winter it would be snowing, other times treacherously icy. In the blackout darkness cycle headlights had to be dimmed so occasionally in the gloom I fell off. Once, the lights failed completely, and I journeyed on in total darkness, eventually being stopped by a local policeman, who, me being an RAF type was sympathetic. On one occasion the chain broke and a remote village workshop had a helpful man who did a repair. Whatever the travel problems, home drew me like a magnet.

On any RAF station an extremely important person was the Station Warrant Officer whose prestige and authority were well above his rank. He had authority and exercised it. The Army RSM (Regimental Sergeant-Major) would have been an equivalent person. The SWO needed treating with respect and avoided when possible.

Each of us in the H-block took it in turn to be room orderly, a duty that included sweeping the floor. One of our airmen found the brush and dustpan routine tedious. He was busily sweeping away, everything going under a loose floorboard, when in walked the SWO and his entourage of NCOs. The lad escaped with the inevitable dressing down, but the Polish airmen in the H-block opposite had their own method of dealing with the SWO, feigning not to understand English. Caught with hands in pockets and forage cap tucked in battledress shoulder lapel, in other words 'improperly dressed', the best move was to say 'No English'.

My only SWO contact was when I called at SHQ for my sweet ration coupons.

Pay parades were something no airman would ever forget. These were held outside. Once one's name was called it was necessary to smartly step forward for a few paces, always saluting before collecting the money, loudly calling out in my case:

'Sir, 731'.

Presumably the officers had their money paid into a bank account. What would have happened if an aircraftman had requested this method of payment?

Apart from receiving our wages Met. Office personnel were involved in few parades, being on shift work was the probable reason. But I was caught for one when I was dragooned ('detailed' was the RAF word) into church. This was a Church Parade for those airmen who were C. of E., when we were paraded to the little village church of Scottow. To me religion was a matter of personal choice and I strongly disapproved of this idea of being forced to take part, so I did not join in the service. A silly attitude, but that was how I felt at the time.

One expression much in use in the wartime forces, spoke of being 'organised'. This basically meant making oneself comfortable, overcoming to some extent the difficulties in way of life imposed by the war. Our Met. Office WAAFs were well-organised. They had hired a houseboat for themselves on the Norfolk Broads at Wroxham where they spent many off-duty hours. It was relaxing and made a welcome break from service life.

Early in the morning our young ladies would search the airfield grass looking for mushrooms for a breakfast fry-up. Somehow they would have 'organised' the means of cooking meals.

The SPs on night duty seemed to have a special relationship with our SHQ billet. Each morning the police came in with an urn of tea and in return I am sure the SHQ staff did favours - quicker shoe repairs perhaps, or the like, all on the basis of being 'well in' with someone.

To me at 18 RAF life was unusual to say the least. This was true when some weeks later I experienced my first RAF Christmas. Each RAF station had on sale its own printed Christmas Cards. On the day itself the Airmen's Mess cooks prepared a special Christmas dinner - turkey with the usual accompaniments, followed by Christmas pudding, beer, minerals, etc. By RAF tradition the airmen were waited upon, the 'waiters' included even the most high-ranking officers. The more forward airmen enjoyed ordering them about, but it was all taken in good part, just for one day only!

CHAPTER 7

Autumn 1944 - Spits, Mossies, Mustangs and Tempests

During the late summer and autumn of 1944 squadrons at Coltishall were to come and go. No. 316 Squadron, known as the 'Warszawski' had been formed in 1941 as a Polish Hurricane Squadron, later flying Spitfires. The Squadron had been at Coltishall in early 1944, then left for West Malling to shoot down V-1s, returning to Coltishall on 27 August 1944, this time flying the American fighter, the Mustang III. In their second stay they were employed doing escort work over W. Europe. Additionally, they escorted convoys and made a general nuisance of themselves along the Dutch coast. From our aerodrome 316 Squadron moved to Andrew's Field, Essex, returning to Coltishall after the war was over.

Two short-stay squadrons were 274 and 80. Both flew Tempest Vs a fast single-seater useful for ground attacks against German airfields and V-2 sites in the Low Countries. Both squadrons had converted from Spitfire IXs in August 1944. The two squadrons operated in tandem, both arriving from Manston on 20 September, leaving for Deurne near Nijmegen - a brief stay, proving the point that squadron personnel were frequently on the move. Both squadrons traced their origins to the end of World War I. 274 Squadron had the motto 'I Overcome', 80 Squadron's was 'Strike True'.

The only Tempests at Coltishall whilst I was there belonged to the two above mentioned squadrons and it was two of 274 Squadron's Tempests that were hit by the Mosquito in the 6 October incident described. Records show that 274 Squadron had already gone to Belgium so why were those two left behind?

602 Squadron ('City of Glasgow') had spent a hectic few months as part of 2nd Tactical Air Force supporting the D-Day operations and the Normandy fighting that followed. On 30 September they came to Coltishall from

Deurne, the idea being to 'rest' the squadron, that is to withdraw it to a quieter area. In fact they were engaged in 'Big Ben' operations which was the code name for attacks against V-2 sites. Flying in a Spitfire XVI one of the young pilots was Raymond Baxter later to become a well-known radio and television commentator on aviation and motoring. A letter I received from him states:

'My Log Book tells me up to three sorties a day were by no means unusual'.

To which I can only add 'some rest!'. The military leadership are famous for such euphemisms, more so now than ever.

On 18 October 602 Squadron left for Matlaske, later moving to Ludham, one of Coltishall's satellite airfields, finally ending the war back at Coltishall. 602 Squadron had been formed in 1925 as an Auxiliary Air Force Squadron. Their badge was a rampant lion and the motto (always in Latin) - 'Beware the tormented lion'.

Another Polish Squadron No. 315 briefly appeared (24 October - 1 November). 315 'Deblinski' Squadron flew Mustang IIIs operating as long-range daytime escorts for USAAF and RAF heavy bombers. Even at this stage of the war Luftwaffe fighters could exact a heavy toll on unescorted bombers over Germany. The Mustangs, although only single-engined, carried external fuel tanks which could subsequently be jettisoned. By this means the range could be greatly extended.

The Polish 303 ('Kosciusko') Squadron was resident for a long period, from 25 September 1944 to 4 April 1945. 303 Squadron flew Spitfires carrying the code letters RF on the fuselage. I passed these so often on my walks to Flying Control that the letters have stayed in my memory.

This squadron had only been formed on 2 August 1940 flying Hurricanes, but was soon in action during the Battle of Britain. In the film of that name a Polish squadron takes part, probably intended to be 303, keen to get into the action in spite of linguistic problems. Now four years later they were flying Spitfires of two different types. The Mark IXs were employed escorting American B-24s (Liberators). These were the bombers we saw in those enormous formations that thundered overhead on the way to enemy territory to attack V-2 rocket installations.

303 Squadron also had low-flying VBs (fighter-bombers). These attacked targets in the Low Countries, dangerous work at low level. In February 1945 the VBs were replaced by Mk XVIs.

On 15 October the Air Defence of Great Britain was redesignated Fighter Command (its former name). It was a name change only since Coltishall stayed in 12 Group.

During late Autumn 1944 I learnt a lesson in my work - namely, to be accurate and always check! Each aircraft carried an altimeter which gave height above ground level, vital knowledge for an aircrew flying at night or even more so, in bad weather. One evening a Mosquito needed a correct ground pressure reading before the altimeter could be adjusted. The aerodrome pressure was known as the QFE, adjusted to sea level it was the QFF. My barometer reading needed to be accurate, but was not. Fortunately my error was noticed. The false reading could have meant the Mosquito being at a lower altitude than the crew anticipated. It was a warning - read, then check. I never repeated the mistake. Other people's lives were at stake.

To return to the Coltishall squadrons. 68 Squadron flew Mosquito night-fighters Mark XIXs and Mark XVIIs (replaced in February 1945 by Mark XXXs). The mark numbers reflected improvements in performance or rôle. I always think of 68 Squadron as being Czech, certainly its motto was in Czech and translated as 'Always ready'. The squadron intercepted Heinkel III bombers that had been converted into flying-bomb carriers launching their V-1s over the North Sea. They also flew patrols along the coast and over the sea, on the look out for intruding Germans intent on attacking RAF aerodromes or returning bombers. 68 Squadron left Coltishall for Wittering on 8 February 1945 then returned from 27 February to 15 March.

125 'Newfoundland' Squadron (motto 'Never to be tamed') like 68 Squadron was a night-fighter squadron basically doing the same military function i.e. counter-measures against V-1s and intruders. They flew Mosquito Mark XVIIs and Mark XXXs and were Coltishall residents from 18 October 1944 to 24 April 1945.

An Australian Squadron, No. 453 was around from 30 September - 18 October 1944. This was another Spitfire 1XB unit, sent to Coltishall to intercept V-1s over the North Sea as well as looking for German intruders. Like most of our Spitfire squadrons they had the occasional go at targets in the Netherlands. The squadron moved to Matlaske. On one occasion I was hitch-hiking when along came a vehicle full of lively Australians wearing the dark blue of the RAAF heading for Matlaske - members of No. 453 Squadron. They gave me a lift.

CHAPTER 8

Ground Defence Course At Church Fenton

From 4 - 15 September 1944 I was temporarily posted to RAF Station, Church Fenton to take part in a ten day Ground Defence Course. The aerodrome was situated between York and Leeds. The aim of the course was to train airmen to defend their own aerodromes.

We studied in some detail the Browning .303 machine-gun. This was the type of weapon used in the turrets of Bomber Command's aircraft all through the war. We were shown how to strip down the gun to the extent that we could identify any faults, the cause of stoppages and how to rectify these. Surprisingly enough, for someone mechanically disadvantaged, all that was said by the NCO instructor made sense and I coped well.

One piece of advice has stayed with me all my life. The first piece of the gun that was removed was placed on a bench, the second piece to the right of it, then the third and fourth and so on. When we assembled we simply put the parts together in reverse order. Simple, but so orderly and effective.

Towards the end of the course we were taken to the butts to fire a Browning, just a short burst with a weapon that fired twenty rounds (bullets) per second.

Aircraft recognition figured prominently in our training and once again my hobby came in useful. I scored highly in a test. My score beat that of an ex-Spitfire pilot - perhaps that was why he was no longer flying! I was rather pleased to have beaten someone wearing those coveted pilot's wings, though I felt that he should have been able to identify aircraft correctly for his own safety when flying.

We had a session in the Dome Trainer. This, as its name suggests, was a dome-shaped building. Inside, a film was projected onto the curved walls, showing the sky and a succession of various types of aeroplanes flying in various directions and with different angles of approach. The idea was to fire a simulated machine-gun at German aircraft, including the Junkers 87 Stuka dive-bomber. 'Hits' were registered and the whole thing was most realistic. The trainer, with correct visual and sound effects, was to me virtually a teenage toy. I could have become hooked on this (by 1940s standard) piece of sophisticated equipment. To my regret only one session was allocated.

At the conclusion of the course we were told our grades and mine was distinction, my first ever in anything - and also the last! We were given one course-free day and on my own made my first ever visit to York, a lovely city and with such places as Bath, Chester (not to mention Norwich!) one of the finest in England. In a bookshop I bought a copy of Battle of Britain pilot Richard Hilary's 'The Last Enemy'. This is a wonderfully moving book.

Returning to Coltishall, once in the billet I stupidly mentioned my distinction and to use the RAF expression was promptly 'shot down in flames'. One of my barrack mates, he who used to tell me how warm his bed was as I set off in the cold to do a night duty, called me a so-and-so young fool. This older man, who pre-war had worked on the 'News of the World', told me my reward for high course marks at Church Fenton would be a prompt transfer to the RAF Regiment. The latter were in effect the RAF's soldiers responsible for aerodrome defence as well as other duties. They wore khaki uniforms, but had blue shoulder flashes and eagles.

Needless to say I did stay in meteorology and did not get transferred to the RAF Regiment. However, I did decide to keep my teenage mouth shut concerning any further military achievements, limited as they would likely be. 'Shooting a line', the RAF expression for boasting, did not go down too well amongst the older men. I was learning.

It had been a pleasant stay at Church Fenton, a good atmosphere and a congenial group of men, both instructors and instructed. Strangely, even after all these passing years, I look back on some RAF units with happy memories, others with indifference or hostile thoughts.

CHAPTER 9
Winter 1944 - 1945 At Coltishall

One night during the winter of 1944-45 some Halifax bombers of 432 (Leaside) Squadron of the Royal Canadian Air Force were operating over Germany. Owing to adverse weather conditions over their own aerodrome, East Moor in Yorkshire, on their return they could not land there. They were diverted to Coltishall where heavy four-engined bombers did not normally land since we had no concrete runways. But the Halifaxes made it and I remember chatting to a young air gunner, English not Canadian, of about the same age as myself. On request he showed me over his Halifax and I remember the fuselage had bullet or shrapnel holes, jagged and sharp.

Some of the Coltishall WAAFs became friendly with the 432 Squadron air crews and some kept in contact after the squadron had returned to East Moor a day or so later. After a time some, inevitably, were shot down over Germany and crew members were listed as missing. This in the end usually meant killed, since only a small proportion of those shot down became prisoners of war. The chance of escape from a Halifax was greater than it was from a Lancaster. The figures quoted are often given as 25 per cent for the Halifax and 15 per cent for a Lancaster. The Lancaster escape hatch was less easy to squeeze through wearing a parachute and thick flying suit. Did 'my' young air-gunner survive? He had looked so slightly built (an advantage in a gun turret) fresh-faced and so very young. What a tragedy that so many of these young men in their late teens and early twenties were killed before life had really begun.

Another incident caused some amusement. One of our Met. WAAFs, an attractive little person named Mollie, had spent a day or so in the company of an American 8th Air Force pilot. Wishing to return her safe and sound before the expiry of her leave pass he resolved to bring her back in style using his giant B-17 (Flying Fortress to us) as an air taxi. Totally without authorisation, and without the duty FCO's permission, the B-17 made its approach.

Our FCO was occupied with our own Spitfires and Mosquitos and over the radio tried to dissuade the B-17 pilot. The latter ignored the FCO, came in, made a safe landing then taxied away from the runway to a spot on the perimeter. Mollie stepped out, so having safely delivered his girlfriend, the pilot took off again, to the consternation of the FCO. Amusing, yes, but good for Anglo-American relations - well, no.

When 'planes were taking off or landing a number of vehicles were always at readiness, just in case of a mishap. There would be a crew on the crash tender, a fire-engine and one usually called the 'blood waggon' (ambulance). Flying Control had their own van, painted bright yellow and known as the 'Yellow Peril'. One day an entire squadron of Spitfires, a dozen or so, flew around unable to land because of two stray dogs on the airfield. The 'Yellow Peril' was sent out to scare off the canine intruders.

One episode stays with me. I remember a young pilot of a Spitfire excitedly bounding into the Met. Office. He had just come back from a sortie over the Netherlands and quite naturally was on a high, glad to still be alive. He told of his exploits and how he had shot up a locomotive. What about the crew, came into my mind? My own father was a steam locomotive driver and it struck me that the driver and fireman were probably Dutch workers anyway. I kept my thoughts to myself. It wasn't me that was being told about the incident, me a mere AC.

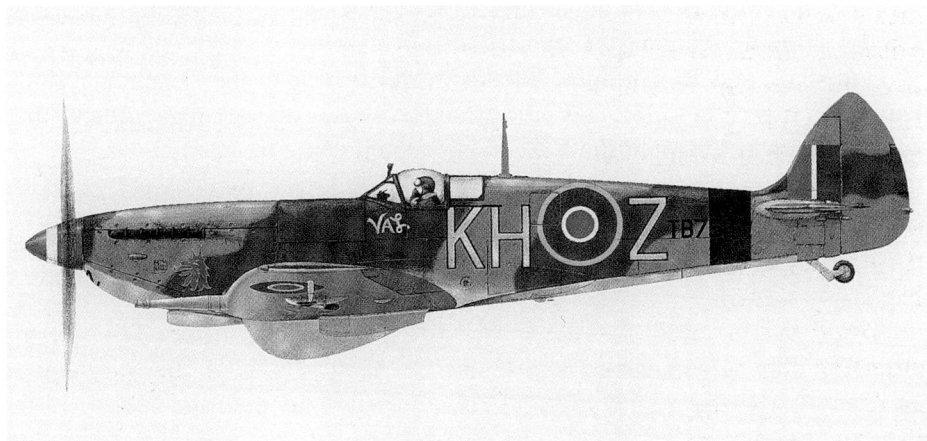

The Manston Spitfire Mk XVI

On 2 December 1944 229 Squadron with their Spitfire XV1E aircraft returned to Coltishall, but on 2 January its Spitfires and some members of the ground personnel were taken over by 603 (City of Edinburgh) Squadron. They were employed doing fighter-bomber sweeps over the Netherlands. 603 Squadron stayed until 24 February 1945 when they moved to our satellite, Ludham. 229 Squadron ceased to exist and has never been re-formed.

603 Squadron had taken part in the Battle of Britain and one of their Spitfire pilots had been Richard Hilary, author of the book I had bought in York. In 'The Last Enemy' he describes his Battle of Britain experiences. He was shot down, badly burnt on his face and hands, which were rebuilt by the famous plastic surgeon Robert McIndoe. Sadly, after a courageous return to operational flying, Richard Hilary was killed in 1943.

On 21 January 1945 a detachment (part) of a squadron of Mustang 1s arrived to do armed reconnaissance patrols over the Netherlands. By this time of course France and Belgium had been liberated hence my frequent mention of the Netherlands. This detachment was part of 26 Squadron. The length of their Coltishall stay is not clear.

No. 124 Squadron equipped with high-flying Spitfire IXEs was at Coltishall from 10 February to 7 April 1945. This unit was known as the 'Baroda' squadron. The badge showed an Indian mongoose and the motto was 'Danger is our opportunity'. The Maharaja of Baroda was a fabulously wealthy man. Did he fund the squadron's aeroplanes? During World War Two RAF aeroplanes were sometimes sponsored and named after the donor.

Once at Coltishall they began attacking rocket sites in the Netherlands and also did shipping reconnaissance sorties.

Coltishall, and its satellite Ludham, were so near to the Dutch V-1 sites that they were the ideal aerodromes for these operations. Once the Netherlands was liberated the V-2 attacks would come to an end.

CHAPTER 10
'Operation Gisela' - The Luftwaffe's Last Fling

On the night of the 3/4 March the Luftwaffe returned in full force (or as much as it could muster) over Britain for the last time. The raid code-named 'Gisela' had been planned for weeks. The intention was to wait for a suitable night, infiltrate a returning RAF bomber stream, then attack the RAF aircraft over bases in eastern and northern England. The RAF bomber force on this particular night consisted of 785 aircraft, the main targets being a synthetic oil-refinery at Kamen, near Dortmund and also the Dortmund-Ems Canal. To attack when bombers were nearly home was when crews could be vulnerable. After a cold operation over Germany the weary crews could perhaps be a little off guard, relieved to have survived and be nearly home in one piece.

I was on night duty on the 3/4 March 1945 and next day in my illegally kept diary recorded:

> 'Was on duty until 8 o'clock this morning. The Luftwaffe returned after midnight for the first time in any force since last June. They were mixed types mostly intruders, and very few bombs were dropped. Mainly confined to East Anglia there were however some other parts of England affected. Several came over our 'drome and 68 squadron were 'up top' fighting them and they scored two successes and one probable was claimed.'
>
> After midnight we had a Mosquito 'prang' at Buxton, bursting into flames and the two fellows were killed - that 'plane was from Great Massingham.
>
> At 03.40 one of 68's Mossies 'pranged' at Stratton Strawless, again the two fellows being burnt to death. I heard one speaking over the R/T a few seconds before he was killed, poor devil.

We had our lights out part of the time owing to the raiders who, incidentally, were out in strength estimated at over one hundred, and they destroyed several of ours, twelve at least. The remainder of this exciting day I have passed sleeping until about one o'clock, had dinner, back to bed again, reading papers, then to tea. And so to bed once more.'

Official German records showed the loss of twenty-one Junkers 88 night-fighters. Three crashed over the UK, four came down in the North Sea, one in the Ijsellmeer, one was shot down over Emden and twelve crashed whilst landing at their Dutch bases. Eleven others were damaged. 142 Junkers 88s took part.

The RAF lost eight aircraft over Germany and the North Sea and twenty were shot down over the UK by the Ju88s, thirteen of these being Halifaxes.

'Gisela' occurred on (for Britain and Germany) the two thousandth night of the war. In all, the night's operations cost the lives of 98 RAF aircrew and 46 Germans - 144 grieving families.

The 03.40 hours incident was due to engine-failure whilst returning to Coltishall. The crew members were F/O Aust (pilot) and F/O Halestrop (wireless operator).

On the 5 March I recorded:

'Another of our Mosquitos crashed yesterday evening, at Potter Heigham, so I am told.'

This aircraft also belonged to 68 Squadron and had been shot down by what, in later times, would be euphemistically called 'friendly fire'. Wonderful military jargon - rather like the 'collateral damage' when civilians are killed by bombs that miss a military target. The 68 Squadron Mosquito it was believed had been shot down by anti-aircraft fire, the aircraft crashing at Grange Farm, Martham, the crew were believed to have successfully baled out (no need to eject in those far-off days).

Also entered in the diary (5 March):

'At 15.30 hrs. a Mosquito of 125 Squadron came over base with only one wheel down. He circled several times trying to get the other down, but gave it up in disgust and came in to land. His other wheel cracked up and so he made quite a good landing in spite of damaging nose, props etc.'

- a successful landing by the pilot of Mosquito HK 287.

The pilot's circling would have had a secondary purpose, to use up surplus fuel in case of a bad crash.

9 March entry:

> *'Early duty until lunchtime with Mr Appleton and after lunch with Mr Crinson. Our Spits have been bombing over Holland today. One came back today with his undercarriage up and another Spit circled round with him to encourage him. He decided eventually to crash-land across the runway for fear of damaging it for other 'planes and found on landing that his wheels were down.*
>
> *The Polish W/Co was seen to bale out over the Hague yesterday evening.*
>
> *We are now across the Rhine and Cologne - or all that remains of it - is now ours.*
>
> *Ted White was posted today to Western Europe.'*

I remember nothing of this Ted, yet he must have made an impression. At this time I wished I could be posted to 2nd TAF (Second Tactical Air Force). This would ultimately have meant being based in Germany, something I wanted.

Next day one of 68 Squadron's Mosquitos overshot the end of the runway and ended up in a ploughed field. This was just one week's air activity on one aerodrome.

CHAPTER 11
Last Days At Coltishall And A Lively Ending

Both the V-1 launching ramps and V-2 pads, plus adjacent equipment and personnel, had been under almost continuous attack, weather permitting, during my service period at Coltishall.

When on night duty one of my dawn tasks was to take a chinagraph map to the office of one high rank officer. This could have been the office of the CO Group Captain A H Donaldson. He was seldom present so in his absence I took the opportunity to have a furtive glance at all his many wall maps and statistics showing such things as a daily tally of V1's shot down.

At this time some of our pilots had developed a technique, daring though dangerous, of flying alongside the V-1s. The Spitfire's wing-tip would be positioned under that of the flying bomb and a sudden movement of the aircraft's wing would flip the missile off course.

The V-1 and V-2 attacks had been from bases in France, Belgium and the Netherlands. Once the Allied Forces had overrun these countries the German vengeance weapon attacks were at an end, the last V-2 falling on 27 March at Orpington, Kent. Poor 34-year-old Ivy Millichamp, a victim of this V-2 was the last British civilian to be killed by German air attack. In all the V-2s had killed 2,754 civilians in Britain with 6,523 seriously injured. Antwerp, the Belgian port, had also been under attack and suffered badly.

As already mentioned Heinkel IIIs were launching V-1s over the North Sea. This was to circumvent the south coast defences. Flying at low-level, mainly at night, the Heinkels were not at all easy to detect. But two Coltishall Squadrons, 68 and 125, had some success against these bombers. They also did night patrols against the occasional conventional bombers and Ju88 intruders making the short trip over the North Sea.

Diary entry 17 March 1945:

> *'Fred and I were on duty together and after tea went to the*

cinema, the film being 'Song of Bernadette' which was really most moving. The warning went towards the end of the film and just before coming out bombs were dropped very near. Walked to the Church Army for supper and then to the office as Fred had left his fountain-pen there. We were almost in the billet when an enemy intruder power-dived to about 200-300 feet and proceeded to fire his cannon at the Church Army van passing by the Guardroom. He also hit one of the bomb-disposal billets, a cannon-shell landing in one chap's bed. The bomb we heard was dropped on the outer circle and aimed for the new CS sign. The 'plane which came over we heard later had been stooging around for an hour while our Mosquitos were patrolling over the North Sea. A lively evening, especially when that fellow swooped down and the guns blazed away regardless.'

The latter quaint expression was typical RAF slang of that period along with wizzo (good), gong (medal), prang (crash) and all the other service jargon that sprinkled our language. 'Dictionary of RAF Slang' (Eric

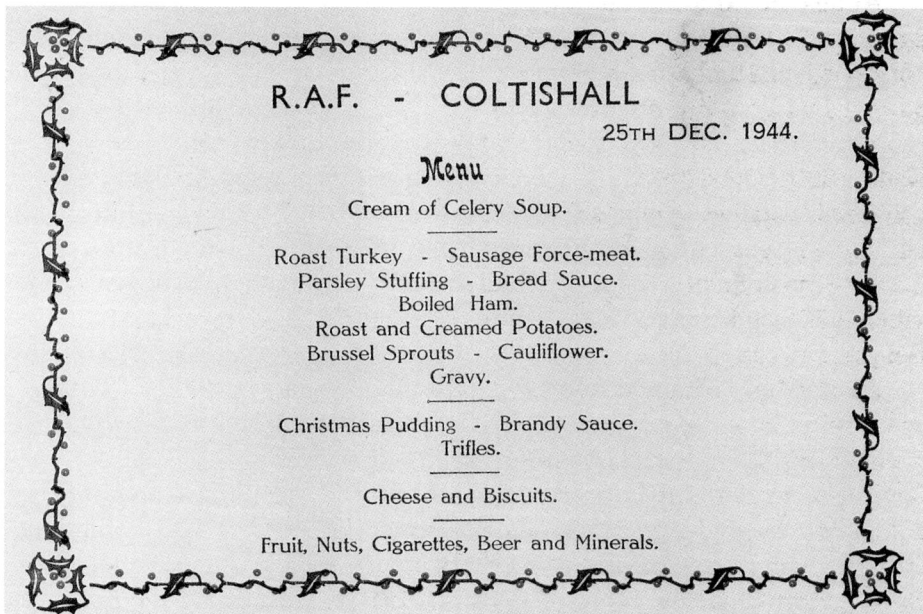

R.A.F. - COLTISHALL

25TH DEC. 1944.

Menu

Cream of Celery Soup.

Roast Turkey - Sausage Force-meat.
Parsley Stuffing - Bread Sauce.
Boiled Ham.
Roast and Creamed Potatoes.
Brussel Sprouts - Cauliflower.
Gravy.

Christmas Pudding - Brandy Sauce.
Trifles.

Cheese and Biscuits.

Fruit, Nuts, Cigarettes, Beer and Minerals.

Airmen's Mess Menu RAF Coltishall Christmas Day 1944. Not a typical meal!

Partridge) records them all.

The Luftwaffe attack was made by a Junkers 88, one of eighteen that had made a fruitless journey because less than 200 RAF bombers were operating over Germany that night.

Initially Fred and I had thought the Ju88 was one of our Mosquitos coming in to land. Once the firing started we knew otherwise and dived into our H-block like a couple of frightened rabbits.

The limited raids of that night, mainly over East Anglia, would probably have been the penultimate attack by the German Air Force against the UK. The long air war, which had caused the deaths of 60,595 civilians in Britain, was mercifully almost at an end.

Diary 18 March:

> *'Fred and I were on early duty together again today. Most of our interest has been occupied by 124 Squadron taking part in a big show over Holland this afternoon at 13.00. They were attacking V-1 sites with light bombs which is typical of their work these days.'*

Diary 21 March:

> *'One of our Spits came down in the sea this morning only two miles off the Dutch coast. German coastal guns drove off both a Walrus and a Catalina trying to rescue the pilot. He was finally captured by the Germans. 124 Squadron wanted to shoot up the coastal guns, but permission was refused.'*
>
> Both the Walrus and Catalina were amphibious aircraft. Being able to land on the sea as well as on land they were ideal for air-sea rescue work. The Germans, however, knowing that a rescued pilot lived to fight another day, decided he was better off in a prisoner-of-war camp; luckily only for a few weeks.

The same day I recorded:

> *'One of 125 Squadron last night shot down one of the few Jerries over attacking objectives with cannon fire. Matlaske, Foulsham and Watton were affected.'*

This particular Luftwaffe aircraft, a Junkers 188 was the last aircraft to be shot down by fighters defending Britain. The crew, Flight-Lieutenant Kennedy and Flying-Officer Morgan, had seen their victim enveloped in flames before plunging into the North Sea. The raid had been the last over the UK.

Next day a B-24 crashed within sight of our aerodrome. Two of the crew were seen to parachute down. Our crash crew was sent to the scene. This particular aircraft had a crew of twelve of whom four bailed out, the rest unfortunately being killed.

On the night of 23/24 March I was on duty with F/O Appleton. Some time before dawn he was told about an airborne force which was to be dropped as a bridgehead the other side of the River Rhine. This news was passed on to me.

Up to this time British, American and other Allied Forces had been slowly, and at a terrible cost, advancing towards the western side of the Rhine. Had I been a soldier I might well have been one of them. One of my schoolmates had been killed in Germany just a fortnight before the end of fighting in Europe.

At 07.30 hrs. a number of aircraft towing gliders came over, just a tiny part of a vast armada of 1,050 aircraft tugs and 1,305 gliders. This force assembled over Belgium. In addition 1,795 troop-carrying transport aircraft carried 8,000 paratroops, plus equipment. On the eastern side of the Rhine, near the town of Wesel, 22,000 men were to be landed.

That afternoon, while thousands of young men were fighting for their very lives, two of us were at the Station Sports Section doing archery. How bizarre war can be. By the time we left the NAAFI that evening 1,100 of those young men had been killed and 1,800 wounded. One in seven had become casualties in half a day's fighting. Much more bitter fighting was to follow before Hitler's Third Reich was finally defeated.

Looking back I realise that March 1945 was one of the most eventful months in my life. To be honest it was exciting, there was a sense of being part of history, which is not intended as a glorification of war. Furthermore, had I been at the sharp end as many of my age were, I would have been scared stiff. Those who were, often have no wish to talk about it, let alone set down their thoughts and feelings on paper as I have done.

On 13 March I was notified that I was being sent temporarily to one of the aerodromes to the north of Newcastle - either to Acklington or Eshott. An airman there had personal family problems to sort out and was being given a few weeks compassionate leave, which the RAF gave when justified.

I cannot say I was pleased about it. Coltishall suited me fine since apart from being near my home I liked the people with whom I lived and worked. Having mentally accepted it, the whole idea was scrapped, and I stayed where I was, to my relief.

On 25 March my diary recorded:

> *'Two Liberators crashed in mid-air complete with full bomb load only half a mile or so from camp. There was a terrific noise as one 'plane dived straight into the ground and exploded. The other one had its tail-unit cut off and also exploded. I watched a tail float down and also one of the crew who had I believe baled out of the tail. Several of the bombs went off a matter of minutes after the crash. Most unfortunate, but several of the crew parachuted to safety.'*

The two American B-24s of 392 Bombardment Group based at Wendling near East Dereham, had collided in dense fog whilst assembling into formation before joining a 1,000 bomber attack on seven oil plants and a tank factory in Germany.

Only two men in each B-24 survived, sixteen being killed. Because of the poor visibility the aircraft were flying 'blind' and it is believed that over Coltishall their wing tips touched. One crashed at Buxton Lammas, the other not far from Skeyton's 'Goat' public house.

I often wondered what happened to the survivors and in 1991, via an American Veteran's Association, traced the whereabouts of two of them. One of them was Harold Hutchcroft from Iowa, with whom I have since corresponded.

The 25 March also had this entry:

> *'One of our Spitfires dropped its bombs over Holland today and returned to have a look, being blown up by its own bombs.'*

Some of our fighter-bomber Spitfires carried a 500lb bomb under the fuselage and one 250lb bomb slung under each wing. Perhaps the pilot was carrying delayed action bombs. Whatever his problems he became yet another casualty.

Another Spitfire pilot was killed flying into a cumulo-nimbus cloud. These enormous thunder clouds with rising up-currents of air could batter a small aircraft, rendering it uncontrollable. Even discounting enemy action there were so many ways of meeting an untimely end. It was generally reckoned that non-enemy crashes took place roughly in the proportions one-third on take-off, one-third on landing and one-third in the air, collisions accounting for some of the latter.

My days at Coltishall were now numbered. On 8 April when reporting for duty, I was given the news, not totally unexpected, that I had been posted overseas. There was an inevitability about it as this was what we had been trained for, yet it came as a slight shock nonetheless. I did my shortest duty ever (17.00 - 20.00) when the senior officer, F/Lt. Anderson, said I could go.

Where would I be going? The Middle East was possible, though the Far East (India or Burma) was more likely. But first I had to be passed as fit for overseas service. I had little doubt on that score, but presented myself for what I expected would be a thorough check. It wasn't. The MO was a Pole and after asking if my feet were all right he then produced his stethoscope and after a quick check pronounced me fit. I was also given an inoculation. Then followed a mad rush round the aerodrome on my cycle, clearance chit in hand, visiting the various sections just to make certain from the RAF viewpoint that I was not making off with any Air Ministry property. The odd Spitfire? Then to crown it all, followed an unwanted evening duty, my last.

On 10 April, 'clearing' finished and farewells said, I set off for the railway station at Felmingham, wobbling my way with kitbag slung across the handlebars. Arriving home I broke the news that I was on a fortnight of embarkation leave.

During my leave I visited my widowed grandmother, aged 82, living at Swaffham. This town was my birthplace and here I had spent almost all of my life save for a few months. Would this be the last time I would ever see my grandmother? Would she still be around on my return? My loveable granddad had died when I was only nine.

On leave I always had the habit of counting off the days - only three to go…. and so on. My morale dropped with each succeeding day until finally I was down to an early breakfast, said my sad farewells, picked up my kit and left just as millions of others had done in mankind's succession of wars. How many years later would I return? Thousands before never did come back. What a waste of lives and what cruelty to those left behind.

It was not until I arrived at Morecambe, Lancs that I would know my overseas destination - S.E. Asia. I had told my parents that before leaving Britain I would let them know in coded form in a letter where I was being sent. An unusual sentence would appear and the first letter of each word would provide the clues. Since we knew no one of that name I chose *'Is Ned down in Aldershot?'* - not exactly cryptology up to Station 'X' Bletchley Park standard! It sufficed. But although a port in India was to be our voyage terminus would I end up in Burma?

CHAPTER 12
Destination India on the 'Chitral'

I reported to a unit at Morecambe, the tortuous journey by rail via Peterborough, Rugby, Crewe and Lancaster being a slow, miserable one. We were allocated billets in private houses, mine being at 25, Westminster Road.

We spent six days at Morecambe marching around, most of our blue kit handed in and, significantly this, khaki drill kit issued in its place. Clearly we were not joining the RAF base in Iceland! What a dreary place poor Morecambe was. Like all British towns it looked worn, drab and tatty after six years of war. Some attempt was made with brush and paint to smarten things up. It was wretchedly cold for April, there was even snow and in the distance could be seen the attractive snow-capped peaks of the Lake District.

On one occasion, as we marched through the town, someone started whistling 'Cavalry of the Steppes' one of the Russian tunes that had become familiar. Soon everyone joined in and it must have sounded like a Red Army unit on the march.

Our reporting point each morning was a theatre. This had a balcony where other ranks sat with the NCOs down below. One lad threw down a penny (large coins in those days). It landed near a sergeant who took it all in good part. Soon came more of the weighty pennies, later a lump of wood. Then some half-wit threw down a half brick. The majority seemed to be on a 'high' at thoughts of going overseas. Most would be on a 'low' once in the Atlantic, slumped over the handrails bringing up their food.

Before I left home my mother had given me some of her coconut pyramids and I remember sitting in the billet eating some of these feeling sad and almost literally homesick. This was a poor billet, the food stingily inadequate and the house cold. We supplemented the food by buying that faithful old standby - fish and chips. For warmth we sought the cosiness of one of the cinemas; at least the massed bodies generated some heat.

On 2 May we were awake early, on parade in the dark at 04.25 complete with full kit and on the train by 06.00 hrs. on the first stage of a journey to India. It was a cold old journey, especially going over Shap Fell, made worse by lack of sleep and hunger, my breakfast having consisted of two sausages. The train stopped at Carlisle so we could obtain tea from a platform canteen. Travelling through Dumfries and Kilmarnock there had been some picturesque scenery in the Southern Uplands.

At journey's end, Glasgow, the train went straight onto the King George VI Docks and within minutes we walked up the troopship 'Chitral's' gangplank. 'Chitral' was a peacetime liner of 15,248 tons gross. Pre-war the ship had carried 306 passengers.

Conditions on board appalled me, our sleeping quarters being one of the ship's holds. This was on the waterline and 250 of us were crowded into a small 30 yds x 20 yds space (approximately 27m x 18m). Most of us were to sleep in triple bunks, each lying alongside another triple bunk. In the narrow gangways some were to sleep, naval-style in hammocks. Luckily for me I had a bunk; sleep in those hammocks looked difficult.

In addition to some civilians there were approximately 3,000 soldiers and airmen on board. The Peninsula and Oriental Company received ten shillings (50p) per day for each one of us that they carried. Even at that time this was not a particularly generous payment. One of the ship's crew must have told me the amount.

The organisation at mealtimes was dreadful. We ate on the Messdeck, taking meals in shifts. Initially the food was passed from the end of the table, each helping himself, but in the case of a meat dish the poor fellows at the end received only gravy. After a day or so of this chaos and greed we worked out a system. All the plates were to be placed at the end of the table, the food equally shared, then distributed.

Next day at 16.30 hrs we sailed from Glasgow on an interesting journey down the Clyde. We passed a large number of ships under construction, the shipbuilders on each one giving us a comradely cheer. In 1925 the 'Chitral' had been built at Glasgow and some of the workmen who watched us sail past may well have been employed in her construction. We are talking of the days when one-quarter of the world's merchant fleet flew a British flag. What a contrast with today - shipbuilding so diminished, ships with flags of convenience, British ships with foreign crews.

Passing down the River Clyde we came to Dumbarton. One young airman next to me on deck, told me with tears in his eyes that he could see his home. Some of the scenery was beautiful, before we finally stopped off Gourock anchoring in a bay that some called 'The Tail of the Tides'.

Unbeknown to us a German mine-laying submarine, the U-218, had set sail from Bergen in Norway on 22 March 1945. Its mission was to lay anchored mines off the island of Ailsa Craig in the Firth of Clyde. In all thirteen mines were laid on 18 April. The fishing vessel 'Ethel Crawford' sank in the minefield, ten men being killed. The U-218 had presumably hoped to sink more than a 200 ton fishing boat, clearly hoping to destroy one or more merchant vessels, troopships or escorts of the Royal Navy. When we eventually sailed through the area some mines had still not been swept. I only knew of the incident from a post-war newspaper sent on to me.

The U-218 returned safely to Bergen on VE-Day so the crew survived the war, unlike the majority. One sad consequence of their final mining operation was the sinking of another fishing vessel the 'Kned' on the 10 July, two months after V-E Day. Of the 37,000 U-boat men around 28,000 were either killed or missing. Here was an attrition rate comparable to that of RAF Bomber Command.

German submarine U-218. Laid mines in the Firth of Clyde, April 1945.

On the 4 May we still lay anchored off Gourock. The ship was crowded and everywhere there were queues, particularly to use the washbasins. The latter were totally inadequate in number and the taps only dispensed salt water for which we used a suitable special soap. There were similar problems to gain a seat in the open-fronted lavatories.

On board, the Queen's band each day gave two entertaining concerts. These I thoroughly enjoyed, being fond of military bands and this was a good one. Some people whiled away the time playing chess or cards. 'Crown and Anchor' was being played for money. Others chatted or read books, in my case a re-reading of 'Pride and Prejudice'. I tried to drum up some political discussion, but to no avail.

On the 5 May we still had not moved. By this time German soldiers en masse were wisely surrendering. It was clear that in a matter of days Germany would be a defeated nation and the infamous Third Reich would fall 988 years short of Hitler's target of a thousand years.

By midnight, however, we had slipped anchor and left Scotland and soon we were in mid-sea passing the coast of Northern Ireland. The movement of the ship was making many of the lads seasick and we saw some peculiar

The 'Chitral' a P&O liner. Carried 306 passengers in time of peace, but 3000 as a troopship.

coloured faces. As for me I felt grim, but managed to keep my food down - just!

The next day we had all settled down into some semblance of a routine though the sea grew rougher and the 'Chitral' was pitching and tossing, the sensation even of walking seemed peculiar.

We were part of a convoy, as far as I could make out, of ten ships. One had steam locomotives on its deck and presented a bizarre sight when at times the engines seemed to be on the sea itself.

At this time I had been detailed to join an important group of men known as the 'A' Deck sweepers. After sweeping this massive deck the rubbish had to be placed in bins. In spite of being warned not to dump our sweepings overboard and have them found by a prowling U-boat, we did occasionally do so if it seemed easier. Once when we attempted the emptying into the Atlantic Ocean, the wind blew the refuse back towards the 'Chitral'. It entered the Officers' Mess Deck via the portholes. This did nothing to increase the popularity of A-Deck's sweepers who were 'requested' over the ship's Tannoy (loudspeaker system) to report pronto to the Ship's Orderly Room to be acquainted with our crimes. At the time I felt it was well worth the ticking-off, class-conscious young devil that I was. In retrospect we were foolish.

We each had a life-jacket which had a small red light attached to it and additionally carried a small tin of chocolate. One day my life jacket vanished, that is, was stolen. I eventually traced it by looking at nearby jackets. I had had the foresight to put my initials in an inconspicuous place and there on a 'friend's' life jacket were my initials which he found difficult to explain. The idea seemed to be with many of them that if someone stole an item of your kit then you 'borrowed' that of someone else.

Had the ship been torpedoed we would have been caught like rats in a trap. One day, well out in the Atlantic, we had lifeboat drill. By the time we had clambered up iron ladders and so forth it took the best past of twenty minutes. It was chaotic, no one seeming to know what was going on. This mass exit would have been worse during the hours of darkness. Should we have had hundreds of men bobbing around in the water wearing life-jackets illuminated by red lights? I just cannot imagine most of us would have made it to a lifeboat or life raft in the darkness.

On the 8 May came V-E Day, the day the nation had longed for, but which for us heading for the Far East and another theatre of war seemed less relevant than one would expect. We were far more concerned with how we felt in the here and now on a ship that rolled ceaselessly as the wind gained in strength.

We did have a thanksgiving service on deck, but the day itself seemed something of an anti-climax and I recollect little of it save for a rumour that the ship would be returning to the UK. Some chance of that!

On 9 May my diary entry was brief:

'Sea rough and food dreadful'.

Certainly there was now more food available, for those of us able to make it to the Mess Deck that is. The absentees' food was now available for those able to face it! The absentees made occasional journeys to the side of the ship sicking their hearts out. Now as far as those rails were concerned it was made crystal clear that if any of us did fall overboard we would stay there. The safety of the troopship would not be compromised in any rescue acts to fish out RAF 'erks' or Army 'squaddies'. A stationary ship was a sitting target for a U-boat's torpedoes.

It continued rough, but relief was at hand since after five-and-a-half days at sea we sighted land. It was the Moroccan coast which, as we neared, appeared both rocky and bleak. The white houses of Tangier glistened in the sunlight and as the ships of the convoy converged at the entrance to the Mediterranean Sea we passed numerous small sailing ships. One mountain peak was covered at its summit by orographic cloud. At least there was now something to look at, unlike the Atlantic which seemed vast in its grey monotony, endlessly stretching to the horizon.

Gibraltar we could only dimly see at a distance and even then it was only just discernible through some thick mist caused at the Straits of Gibraltar, where the comparatively cold waters of the Atlantic met the warmer Mediterranean waters.

Next day, 12 May, we were in safer waters and no longer in convoy. The European part of the war was over, the U-boat danger at an end, so the 'Chitral' sailed on its own, hugging the northern coastline of Africa, which looked in the main bleak and inhospitable. One point of interest was Algiers, passed at 19.30 hrs. It was large and seemingly perched on high ground. That evening there was community singing which continued until dusk which came much earlier than in England. The open deck was pleasant, not so our D5 sleeping deck which was so hot as to make sleeping difficult.

The following day was sunny and an ideal temperature. The clear skies gave the Mediterranean that incredibly picture postcard type of blueness and it was so wonderfully calm. The ship was again sailing within sight of Africa and we passed by Bône (now Annaba) and La Calle. In the distance was Cape Bon, where, in May 1943 the Afrika Korps with its Italian Allies had surrendered. In all, some 150,000 were captured.

The 14 May was another sunny, cloudless day that passed pleasantly listening to the band of the Queen's, talking and reading. On 'A' Deck a concert was given before dusk. We were no longer near land.

Next day in the far distance was Libya. By now almost everyone was wearing tropical kit which made life more tolerable. The washing of clothes was something of a problem, it being so difficult to gain the use of a washbasin. One blessing was the water, now tasting less salty.

A choral entertainment was given the following day, a day that produced a most beautiful moonlit evening for an after-dusk stroll on deck.

After dawn on 17 May we entered the Suez Canal. Seeing Port Said was interesting, but regrettably there was no question of going ashore. I remember little of the city except for the statue of canal builder Ferdinand de Lesseps.

Passing through the canal there was little to see apart from the British Army camps. From the soldiers came shouted insults of which the most printable would be:

'Get some service in', or 'Get your knees brown'.

The mainly good-natured exchanges continued until camp and ship were out of earshot. Each time we came to a camp this happened. I also have a vague recollection of seeing one isolated camel, Egyptians using the canal as a urinal, the crumbling canal banks and the Bitter Lakes where several captured Italian battleships were moored.

During our passage through the canal what there was to be seen was mainly on one side of the ship to which we naturally crowded. This made the 'Chitral' difficult to navigate so an announcement over the Tannoy asked half of us to move to the other side. How we achieved this I cannot say.

After several hours we arrived at Suez, where water and stores were taken on board. Suez harbour offered a fine anchorage being virtually landlocked. Most of 18 May we were anchored off Suez besieged by a number of bumboats, small boats the owners of which were selling a variety of goods, mainly leather craft work. These were hoisted on board in a basket, the money being lowered after a purchase had been made. I bought only one item, a box of Turkish Delight.

After tea we began the last lap of the journey, to Bombay. The 19 May saw us in the Red Sea, heat intense with hardly a breath of wind and the ventilation below decks was totally inadequate. The ship's crew fixed up for our benefit a tarpaulin arrangement to give us more fresh air. This had the appearance of a large, wide elephant's trunk. Unfortunately this was not really effective, so I took my bedding onto the open deck which offered a hard bed, but at least it was marginally cooler than down below.

The following two days were hellish. The heat was intense, reminiscent of opening a hot oven door. We sweated profusely and the food was deadly, both in quality and quantity. There was no way of supplementing one's diet - no NAAFI or Church Army, no fish and chip shop. The one extra source of food was the ship's canteen which sold small packets of biscuits, but these could not last forever.

On 22 May after dusk we passed Aden, but the novelty of the journey had worn off and we hardly cared where we were and just longed to be off the ship. The heat was affecting my skin, probably the repeated perspiration, so I reported sick. The MO was most definite - I had scabies! The suggested treatment was a hot bath, scrub the affected parts, then apply some kind of lotion. At least I gained access to a bath, but the scalding feeling from the lotion was worse than the 'scabies' and the following day the mass of spots were as bad as ever. I itched all over.

During the day I was discussing my 'scabies' with a much-travelled stewardess. She took one look at my spots and told me the MO's diagnosis was utter rubbish and that I had prickly heat which most of us would suffer from in India.

On 26 May we packed our kitbags with real enthusiasm ready for disembarking next day. Anything seemed preferable to the 'Chitral' which, come the great day, we literally staggered off with full equipment. We disembarked with kitbag, webbing, small valise, large pack, water bottle, rolled up gas cape, respirator, sten gun, steel helmet and on the head a ridiculous topee (pith helmet).

At the harbour, within sight of the famous Gateway of India, we were packed into lorries and driven to the Base Reception Centre at Worli, which was part of Bombay. Conditions at Worli, though spartan, were positively luxurious in comparison with the 'Chitral'. The billets were spacious, built of concrete and brick, each housing around a hundred men. Considering the heat they were surprisingly cool. The food - always an important issue - was adequate.

The first evening, four of us set off on an exploratory walk, eventually ending up in side streets away from the central area. Until then I had never witnessed such degradation and squalor. Many of these poor Indians were living in shacks made from beaten out petrol cans or any scrap material available. The smell was unpleasant with deep gutters running along the sides of the streets and full of filthy water. So small were these shanty town dwellings that these desperately poor people did most things outside, even the cooking.

Cows, regarded by Hindus as sacred animals, wandered the streets intermingling with ox-carts and Rolls Royces, street vendors and beggars. The lives of the well-dressed car owners were in complete contrast to those of the poor. Our discoveries abruptly ended when two patrolling military policemen suggested we return to safer main streets, which we did.

The day we arrived we handed in our topees, hundreds of them, and received in exchange a bush hat. The topee episode was a prime example of military waste. Someone in the distant past had received a contract to produce thousands of topees. These were issued in the UK, transported by us to India, handed in, then presumably re-sold as a job lot - or even destroyed. I visualised a topee mountain on fire.

There was little to be done at Worli save wait for a posting somewhere in India - or, even worse, Burma. I had no wish to be too near those little Japanese. In our spare time we had the opportunity to travel into the centre of Bombay which had many cinemas and officially approved restaurants within bounds to British servicemen. To travel into Bombay we used a train, bus or horse-drawn vehicle.

One favourite spot was Breach Candy where there was a swimming pool. Here on 31 May my tour of India could have come to an abrupt close. Attempting to learn to swim, an ability I never mastered, I floundered in a panic and had to be fished out by someone or other.

Within three days of arriving in India at one of the hottest times of the year, our active ranks for the daily parade became depleted. Many of the lads were ill succumbing to heat stroke, sun stroke, dysentery and other afflictions.

On 5 June volunteers were called for to take part in a mercy errand at Bombay Docks. Here we unloaded two long train loads of wounded or ill men, mainly soldiers from Burma. There were many tuberculosis cases, poor fellows also with lost legs. In what an appalling state these men were going home. I silently cursed the war and what it had done to these young men we were stretchering aboard a ship.

The next day my posting came through, to St Thomas Mount, Madras - not Burma!

CHAPTER 13
'Tommy's Bump' Not Burma

On the evening of 6 June gharries (lorries) took us to Central Station where we boarded a troop train on which conditions were fairly comfortable in comparison to some later experiences. All through the night the train frequently stopped. Even in the small hours of the morning each station had vendors selling tea, cakes and fruit. Everywhere there were beggars - men, women and children. Some were lepers, some blind - every form of deformity could be seen and all were begging for food or money. So this was India, part of the British Empire. It was pitiful and once the sheer wretched, hopeless plight of these poor people reduced me to tears. It was heartrending, beyond comprehension.

We journeyed all through the next day, twice stopping at stations for food. In addition we had been issued with boxes of American emergency K-Rations. These contained various items of food, American-style, for which I never acquired a taste. Some, such as the drinks, required hot water which was an impossibility, short of using the locomotive's boiler.

On the morning of 8 June eight of us arrived in Madras, one of them a Lancashire lad, Ken Spencer, who had been with me on the 'Chitral'. The grapevine had it that St Thomas Mount was a good posting and we found ourselves billeted in a thatched hut known as a basha (pronounced 'basher'). The cold showers were clean, also the lavatories - thickly whitewashed and always smelling of chlorine. The food seemed moderately acceptable.

Two of us hitch-hiked from St Thomas Mount to the centre of Madras coming back partly by electric train and partly by rickshaw, which was a novel method of travel. Later I never used a rickshaw, hating the idea of a human between the shafts of a cart pulling me along as I sat in splendour.

Next day I booked in, visiting armoury, sick-quarters, dental section and the rest to obtain the necessary signatures on my arrival chit. This was a sensible system.   That evening I had an unpleasant bout of sickness and diarrhoea which continued most of the next day.   During my tour there were to be many more such episodes.

A 'tour' at this time was four years for a single man and this seemed an eternity of time.   The actual length clearly would depend upon the duration of the war in the Far East.   Japan must be defeated if I was to be in South East Asia Command for less than four years.   Married men did six months less.

The aerodrome was situated seven miles to the south-west of Madras, a city on the coast of the Bay of Bengal.   The name of the RAF station was taken from the nearby hill of the same name and there was also a St Thomas Mount village.   The Mount was the spot to which St Thomas allegedly travelled as a missionary.

The aerodrome, sometimes called 'Tommy's Bump' had been built pre-World War Two.   It had two concrete runways, one of 2,000 yards length and 50 yards width (3,218m x 80m); the shorter one being only 1,500 yards long (2,414m).   The buildings were a mixture of temporary (e.g. our bashas) and permanent such as the two hangars, one always known as the Hart hangar.

The staff of 743 Forecast Centre February 1946. Taken at Madras (St. Thomas Mount). Back row: on left Ron, 3rd Jack, 6th Ken.

My meteorological duties took place in the Control Tower building in which our unit, 743 Forecast Centre, had an office. 743 Forecast Centre consisted of a few officers and several other ranks, initially all British. The officers were mainly ex-grammar school masters and the British Other Ranks (BORs) ex-grammar school boys; this mitigated against promotion compared to some trades.

The met. equipment was poorer than we had used in the UK, but on the plus side the weather was incredibly uniform, monotonously so. In Britain we had recorded variations from hour to hour.

Normally we worked 48 hours in eight days, with one day off in four. Each 48 hour period included one night duty. On these I normally felt at my lowest at around 05.00 hrs., but revived with sunrise. Regarding sunrise and sunset, being only 13 degrees north of the equator, there was little variation in the lengths of day and night, the difference being about two minutes each month. There was a rapid change from night to day and vice-versa and there was virtually no twilight.

My fellow airmen in 743 Forecast Centre were mainly pleasant and the officers civilised, kindly and thoughtful. Working life was not too arduous and the company congenial with the exception of one character. This was the airman who before going off duty scrawled across one of our charts:

'War raises to positions of power the base and the vulgar.'

This, as intended, soon met the gaze of one of our officers who initially accused me. I asked him if he really thought I was that stupid and he said 'No'. The real culprit was never found, though I knew who it was. I am sure it was written in sheer frustration by a thoroughly cantankerous man who also was on the rebellious side, but normally held it in check.

The above-mentioned airman could be both outspoken and witheringly sarcastic as Ken and I quickly found out soon after arrival. The RAF had issued us with an all-purpose knife and a lanyard, so we wore these attached to our bush shirts. Said airman soon spotted us, scathingly remarking:

'Do you two think you're _____ Boy Scouts?'

In our naïve innocence I believe we wore them as a weapon at hand in case of attack by a snake. Needless to add we never wore them again, having made fools of ourselves. Today we would say we were on a learning curve.

Except for occasional breaks at a hill station I must say from the outset I detested the climate of southern India. It was not just hot, it was also so incredibly humid. Essentially there were two seasons - a wet season (the NE

66

Monsoon) from September to January and a longer dry season.

During the 'cool' season (winter) the climate was tolerable, but for most of the year it was hot, even at night, and usually there was high humidity. The climate was enervating in the extreme. When off-duty we spent a considerable part of our time lying on our charpoys (beds), writing letters - or falling asleep. The dampness and heat caused excessive perspiring which damaged cells on the skin's surface. Pinhead sized bumps appeared surrounded by red skin. This caused intense irritation and burning - milaria rubra, prickly heat to us. The neck, chest, back, groin and armpits seemed to be the worst affected parts. Mine only disappeared during the cool season, or on hill party.

Most of us seemed to experience bouts of diarrhoea and as for colds we had as many as in the UK. But the main thing was to avoid the worst medical conditions such as malaria and typhoid.

1945. At the foot of the steps leading to St. Thomas Mount Convent.
Left to right: Ken Spencer, Terry Carnell, Eric Powell, Tom Brabbins, author.

On 24 July a small group of us climbed St Thomas Mount, only 250 ft. high (76m) but it really stood out and overlooked the aerodrome. At the summit in 1547 the Portuguese had built a church. The hill top was, and still is, the home of a Franciscan convent. The nuns looked after abandoned and destitute babies and other children under the age of five. They still continue the same work today.

The only route to the top was by climbing the brick-built steps, constructed in 1728. Today, inevitably, there is a tarmac road for motorists and the steps are crumbling.

At the convent the Mother Superior welcomed us warmly and showed us the buildings and antiquities on display. There was a painting of the Madonna and Child, allegedly the work of Saint Thomas, as was a carved stone. The painting was occasionally said to weep. I'm afraid I was sceptical, but in secret.

Later we had cold drinks in the guest room. Our reception was kindly and gracious and before leaving we signed the visitors' book. A few days earlier another Loveday had signed; the nuns were surprised to entertain another one. Later I met him, but he was not from my part of England.

CHAPTER 14
'Operation Zipper' -
The One That Never Took Place

Long before the European War was over the thoughts of the strategic planners must have turned to the Far East where countries occupied by the Japanese would have to be fought for and liberated. One such country was Malaya. An assault on that country was planned with 9 September 1945 set as D-Day. The invasion plan was code-named 'Operation Zipper'.

A fleet of over 500 RAF aircraft was massed in India, Ceylon (now Sri Lanka) and the Cocos Islands. It was planned to capture Malayan aerodromes such as Kelanang, Port Swettenham and Kuala Lumpur. The latter aerodrome, according to the plan, was to be in our hands by D-Day plus 25 days. By D+28 four squadrons of Mosquito bombers were to fly into Kuala Lumpur aerodrome. The squadrons, all flying Mosquito V1 aircraft, were numbers 45, 82, 84 and 211. All four were at RAF St Thomas Mount for part of the time I was there.

On my arrival day (8 June) the aircraft of 84 Squadron flew in and by 26 June the ground crews of No. 84 had arrived. From December 1942 to October 1944 84 Squadron had flown American Vengeance single-engined bombers over Burma. They then converted to the far superior Mosquito. The Vengeances were then considered obsolete and to be 'disposed of' Curiously enough on one of my explorations of the airfield I came across several Vengeances in large wooden crates, some for wings and some for fuselages. All appeared in mint condition. At the time it struck me as a waste of dollars. But in this I was mistaken. Crews deserved the best aeroplanes available.

Having only taken delivery of their Mosquitos in February 1945 the 84 Squadron pilots were at St Thomas Mount still familiarising themselves with their new aircraft. Fortunately for them the war ended and the planned invasion was unnecessary and on 1 September they flew off to another Indian base, RAF Baigachi.

On 11 July another Squadron arrived, No. 211. They had been flying Beaufighters in Burma, but in May 1945 had been re-equipped with Mosquitos. They were flown to St Thomas Mount from Yelahanka to prepare for 'Operation Zipper'. Their stay was a short one; the war over they left for Siam (Thailand) on 24 September. In my diary I recorded:

'The food is a wee bit improved, probably because 211 Squadron left yesterday'.

So much for 211's departure - to me it simply meant bigger helpings. The squadron, no longer needed, evidently disbanded in March 1946.

On 12 October 1945, 45 Squadron from Cholavarum arrived at St Thomas Mount where it was based until being disbanded (the fate of many squadrons) on 15 March 1946. I have no recollection whether this led to bigger helpings or not!

The ultimate surrender of the Japanese, which I mention later, made the invasion of Malaya unnecessary. Had 'Operation Zipper' taken place I might well have been included amongst the ground staff involved in the invasion, but this is mere speculation.

After the D-Day landing in Normandy, 'Operation Zipper' was the second largest amphibious operation ever planned. I wonder how many lives that one would have cost?

CHAPTER 15

Labour Victory, Hospital and V J Day

It has often been said that the votes of servicemen swept the Labour Party to power in 1945. Certainly on board the 'Chitral' the announcement over the Tannoy loudspeakers that Prime Minister Winston Churchill had resigned was greeted with cheering. The respected wartime leader with V E Day over was no longer wanted. Of my acquaintances on board and also in India later, the majority were either voting Labour or would have done so had they been old enough to vote. I, at 19, was in the latter category. It rankled that although considered old enough to be sent to the Far East I was too young to vote, not being 21. It did not bother me being posted overseas, but the voting business really maddened me.

Polling Day was 6 July, but with all the postal votes to be counted it was 26 July before the first results were announced and these indicated a massive Labour majority. Next day it was a certainty and this was the result on which we pinned our hopes. The fighting was not simply about the defeat of Germany and Japan, it was also about a fairer, more egalitarian Britain. There was now an air of optimism about the reforms ahead, but first Japan had to be defeated.

At this time I was intensely pro-Russian. The USSR was our

The author in India. RAF blue replaced by khaki drill but the forage cap carries on.

71

wartime ally. From 1941-1945 we had admired the heroism and sacrifices of Soviet forces and the civil population in 'The Great Patriotic War'. By bearing the brunt of the land fighting, certainly from 1941-1944, the Russians had indirectly saved British lives on a vast scale.

But for me at this time I was politically naïve enough to believe that Stalin's USSR was a socialist paradise run for the benefit of ordinary people. Older and wiser heads than mine had fallen into this intellectual trap. But once the war was over it took quite a few months before I could see Stalinism as it really was. I believed a socialist Labour Government as the natural ally of communist Soviet Russia. In the early post-war disagreements between the USSR and the West my sympathies were often with the former. I would refer to:

'Lies about Russia' …. 'our greatest ally' and so forth.

I was correct in one thing, Britain's reign as a great power was over. I wrote:

'England is no longer a great power. The nation wore itself out during six years in which it put all its efforts into defeating Germany ..... the USSR and USA are the great powers of the future.'

And so it remained for half a century until the Berlin Wall came down.

On 6 August I began an unexpected spell in hospital. An officer going to Madras city on a motor-bike had offered me a lift. Due to my own awkwardness the heel of my right foot slipped into the rear wheel, removing part of the right shoe, the sock and a lump of flesh. As luck would have it one of our own RAF ambulances was going in the opposite direction and took me to our nearby St Thomas Mount Station Sick Quarters.

In Station Sick Quarters, apart from the discomfort of the injury, I enjoyed a thoroughly pleasant time. The ward was comfortable, well-lit and airy and the food reasonably good. There was abundant time in which to relax, read or write letters. The ward had a cupboard full of magazines such as the long-since defunct 'Picture Post', 'Everybody's' and 'Lilliput'.

My companion in the next bed suffered from recurrent bouts of malaria. He lay on his bed in that heat shivering with cold and the nursing orderlies kept piling on the blankets until he had five or six. I couldn't believe it.

There was no discipline. An orderly came round with mid-morning and mid-afternoon tea and biscuits - even the occasional tot of spirits for which I had no taste. Visiting hours were, within reason, unrestricted and my friends came in when they felt inclined. The orderlies were considerate, one of the Indians being particularly kind, dressing my wound with great care. From time to time the Medical Officer popped in.

Whilst in Station Sick Quarters the war was reaching a surprisingly speedy conclusion. On 6 August 1945 the first atomic bomb was dropped, on Hiroshima.

At the time I wrote:

> *'What would have happened if the Nazis had used it first on us? This new devilish weapon can possibly destroy civilisation unless we learn to live together peacefully. It is something so terrible as to be unimaginable'.*

Three years later I read John Hersey's 'Hiroshima'. It gave in graphic detail an appalling account of what happened to six Japanese living in the city. It was harrowing to read what we had done. It was a cruel act, but certainly saved the lives of thousands of our prisoners-of-war. It must have shortened the war and again saved lives of Allied Servicemen liberating countries such as Malaya and Burma.

On 9 August Nagasaki received the second and last atomic bomb. The same day the USSR, having declared war on Japan, invaded Manchuria. By now the Japanese could no longer continue the war and by 15 August it was over. V-J Day came just over three months after V-E Day, sooner than we had imagined possible.

On V-J Day I was discharged (with no great enthusiasm) from hospital, reported sick next day as instructed, and for 48 hours was excused all duties. Even then it was a considerable time before I could wear ordinary shoes.

Our official celebration of the end of the war came two days later with a good dinner served of course by the officers, a meal of chicken and mixed salad.   The previous evening many BORs had celebrated victory in the canteen by heavy drinking, arguing, fighting, smashing bottles and general mayhem.   The others, the majority, looked on in astonishment.

Peace came as an anti-climax. The war was now over and this was, after all, the main reason for us being sent to the Far East anyway.   The objective having been achieved it now seemed a waste of time. We became fed up, too discontented for our own peace of mind and just longing to go home. Things had now gone distinctly flat.

We were now in a peacetime RAF so discipline began to tighten up. Each week a colour-hoisting ceremony was to be held on the barrack square, a rough, dry, barren piece of ground that once, to the annoyance of an officer, I used as a short cut. At least at Coltishall it had been a clearly delineated square of tarmac, holy ground. At St Thomas Mount it was barely recognisable.

Anyway, the first of these parades took place and was to me hilarious. Nobody knew what to do and the officers clearly had only the briefest acquaintance with the correct procedure. Those on high were not amused by this comic opera shambles that would not have been out of place in 'Dad's Army' to be seen many years later on our television screens. We were ordered to attend three practice parades in one week, all beginning at 07.00. Typically, the parades eventually petered out.

The spotlight was then turned on dress and hygiene. An order was issued that white or coloured shirts were not to be worn either on or off the aerodrome. This had a short-lived run, but was later rescinded. It was decided that we could wear civilian clothing, but only off camp, which seemed fair.

A silly order was issued saying we were to wash regularly and to wear clean clothing. In that damp heat the order was fatuous. In such a greenhouse atmosphere we showered more than once a day and frequently changed into sweat-free khaki shorts and bush jackets.

CHAPTER 16

Bashas, Wild Life and Food at St Thomas Mount

Our billet as I have written was a basha, this being a structure consisting of wooden supports and roof timbers. The sides were filled in with interwoven leaves of palm. The roofs were thatched, again palm leaves being used. There were no glazed windows. The 'windows' were interwoven palm on a wooden frame, the frames hinged at the top and opening outwards. There were eight windows and two doors.

Each basha had a servant or bearer. Ours was a charming Indian who lived locally. For the payment of one rupee (7½p) per week from each of us

Photo taken on steps of barrack block RAF St. Thomas Mount, Madras October 1945. L to R: Terry Carnell, _____ , Jack Loveday, Cpl Miller. At front Ken Spencer.

we had our billet swept, shoes cleaned, water fetched from a nearby well and dirty clothing taken to the dhobi-wallah (washerman or woman).

We each had a supply of surprisingly cold water. 'Joe', as we called our bearer, obtained chatties for us. A chatty was a narrow-necked porous pot. By throwing water onto the outside of the chatty, by a process of evaporation the water inside was cooled. During daytime the hut bearers acted as property guards.

Joe made the best cold drinks I have ever tasted. He made a lime drink using the real fruit, for which he charged us one anna a beaker (roughly 1p). Had we really got to know Joe, who had a wife and family, I am sure we would have found him a delightful man. Apart from the language barrier we basically did not bother.

Our bashas had been built in a small area of woodland, trees well spread out and of unknown species. One particularly attractive tree had pretty red blossoms. Wildlife was in abundance - the occasional dog, several cats, the odd cow, a monkey, squirrels, frogs, bats, lizards and a few score BORs! There was a goat who enjoyed our banana skins and eventually produced kids. Occasionally scorpions appeared, though I never saw one. Once I watched a chameleon changing colour as it moved round a tree. The praying mantis with its long, thin body and large bulbous eyes was a curious insect. It held its forelegs in an attitude of prayer and always fascinated me as did a curious worm-like creature with four short legs. We called it a snake-leader.

Rats used to enter the basha and seemed omnivorous. Tablets of toilet soap, clothing, food, newspapers - all seemed acceptable. I mistakenly left a peanut in the pocket of a khaki bush shirt and had an inside pocket gnawed through.

Two birds, the crow and the kite hawk, were always well in evidence, the latter I believe ornithologists refer to as the pariah hawk. The crows were constantly flying in and out of the open-windowed cookhouse. One morning one of our lads whilst using the tea urn took his eyes off his plate only to lose his slice of bacon to a hungry crow. To our amusement he accused everyone on our table.

Once the meal was over scraps of unwanted food were always scraped into an outside swill bin. Kite hawks always perched in the nearby treetops, their sharp eyes on the look-out for any savoury tit-bits. They would swoop with unbelievable dexterity and speed to snatch with their talons any scraps of food on exposed plates. We soon realised plates had to be carried in one hand and covered with the other. New arrivals from the UK were usually allowed to find out the hard way about the dive bombers. These birds fulfilled the useful role of scavengers.

Flies, particularly the small mango flies, were a pest by day being so fond of our eyes. The main dusk to dawn enemy was the mosquito, though luckily the aerodrome itself was reasonably free of malaria. After dusk, to avoid mosquito bites, we were under orders to have our sleeves rolled down and to wear khaki drill trousers instead of shorts.

Late evening and night duties were a pain. Our well-lit office attracted mosquitoes, flies, flying beetles and a wide variety of insects never seen in the UK. Off the aerodrome it would have been worse with stagnant water and refuse as breeding grounds for insects. In that respect our aerodrome was relatively clean. Outside the office by night we heard crickets and the distant jackals hunting in packs.

With sunrise the worst of the insect invasion would be over and it was the turn of the barking dogs and the pleasant dawn chorus of smaller birds to which our resident crows and kites made no contribution.

Regarding the pariah kites, one day with my friend Ken, I was sunbathing on top of a flat-roofed barrack block. A kite swooped down, landing on Ken's head. Understandably, since these birds had a wing span of one metre, we never used the roof again.

We were issued with mosquito-nets which were tied to wires running through the billet at a little above head height. By day the nets were hung on the wires, but at night the nets were tucked under the bed clothes. There was a nightly ritual of lifting the net and examining the bed before entering it just in case a snake had slithered inside it. The one we feared was the poisonous Krait. Any snakes we did see were usually a few feet long and non-poisonous. One of our airmen found a snake coiled behind a toilet and made a swift exit in record time.

The mosquito nets did have the effect of restricting any movement of air since the mesh was so fine. Often the humid heat would be so insufferable that we threw the nets back and risked the consequences. Soon after arriving in India we had been issued with mepacrine anti-malaria tablets, but these were reputed to make the skin turn yellow so we stopped taking them.

The charpoy or 'charp' was a curious type of bed. It consisted of a wooden frame, but our bodies rested on a criss-cross web of thin ropes. Since we only had a minimal amount of bedding underneath us we often woke up showing rope marks. This back pattern was known as a 'charpoy rash'.

By and large we were not a badly treated bunch of young men. Our living conditions were worse than that of our RAF colleagues back in the UK, yet in comparison to what soldiers had had to put up with in say the Western Desert or a Burmese jungle we were living an easy life. But all servicemen by tradition have a grumble.

One constant source of complaint was the food. We ceaselessly moaned about it and, in view of the fact that the war was over, quite justifiably. Had we been inmates in one of H.M. Prisons we could not have fared much worse.

The Airmen's Mess, aptly named, was a foul building being hot, stuffy and sticky. The windows because of the heat, had to be kept open and birds constantly flew in and out, hardly hygienic. We sweated so profusely that we tended to bolt down our food to get out quickly, a habit that remained with me for years. The Mess was fly-ridden, crowded and stank!

There were three meals a day. Breakfast at 07.00 hrs. almost invariably included a large duck egg - fried, usually half cold and greasy. The tinned bacon was served in mangled small pieces, more fat than lean. After a time I could no longer face those duck eggs.

Tiffin, the midday meal, usually consisted of corned beef in many guises - straight from the tin, mashed, fried or cooked in batter. Sometimes we had spam. To round off the meal we had a mango which I found sickly and sweet, so after a time they received the duck egg treatment.

Dinner was at 17.00 and often the main course would be fat, stringy meat. This was accompanied by either a minuscule quantity of whole fresh potatoes or large quantities of the reconstructed mashed variety. Sometimes we had tinned meat and vegetables, known to us as Maconochie's M and V. Fresh vegetables were rare. Our alternative was small quantities of tinned carrots or runner beans. Just occasionally there would be a salad.

The bread was usually tolerable, though the ex-USA butter had a rancid taste. Bread was rationed at one stage, though not, so we were told, for the officers and sergeants - not a morale booster.

To summarise, if at St Thomas Mount the food was good then there was little of it, but if available in quantity it was of poor quality. Did it have to be so poor? One airman thought not. He had been a gardener in 'civvy street' and took an interest in local Indian food prices. His investigative work uncovered a 'scam'. He asserted that in the case of, say tomatoes, double the price actually paid was being drawn from RAF funds. Those in authority requested his immediate posting, 'whistle blowers' not being wanted. He was in fact posted, but when last heard of was about to be demobbed under Class 'B' release. His horticultural expertise was of greater value in the UK than to the RAF.

Some evenings I managed to refuel at the RAF canteen run by a local Indian contractor. At the canteen two fried eggs (from a hen not a duck!) and chips could be bought for six annas (2½p). Outside the aerodrome boundary was Azad's, a canteen inspected and approved by our medical staff, so it was safe to buy their cooked meals, ice-cream and cold drinks.

Occasionally, in Madras I would go to a Chinese restaurant which, like Azad's, was RAF approved. At one establishment 'My Coffee Bar' I was introduced to the delights of iced coffee. It was necessary to be ultra-careful buying food and drinks, so many outlets being unhygienic. I had no wish to become ill or worse. Only once, months after, whilst in northern India, did I buy a drink from a source not officially approved. I had a desperate thirst and bought a cold drink from an Indian vendor on a railway station platform. I suffered pangs of doubt for days afterwards.

I used to spend at least one-third of my pay at Azad's and the aerodrome canteen, not to mention peanuts, oranges and bananas from the camp fruit wallahs. Even so, I occasionally fantasized about food, high on my list being fresh vegetables, apples, bread and cheese with pickled onions, not to mention Shredded Wheat with fresh cold milk.

In spite of my criticism the catering staff did us proud on Christmas Day 1945. Even a menu was printed, which shows a dinner consisting of roast turkey, roast beef, peas, Brussels sprouts, roast and boiled potatoes. This was followed by Christmas pudding and brandy sauce, cheese and biscuits, plus drinks. All this fare served by the officers of course. Some of the latter were the worse for wear, even the CO being 'lively'.

Tea consisted of salad, jam tarts, cakes and mincepies, but no officers as waiters.

CHAPTER 17

Entertainment at St Thomas Mount : Indians

As far as entertainment was concerned we fared quite well at St Thomas Mount. The Station Cinema was well-attended and had frequent changes of programme, the only drawback being the necessary breaks each time a reel was changed. There were also other breakdowns that had the intolerant and boisterous audience at their noisiest. We always watched the films whilst eating - usually bananas, oranges and peanuts.

The cinema became a source of strife between the senior officers and ourselves. We were dead awkward, all part of our class-conscious 'them and us' attitude. The end of the programme was the signal to stand to attention for the National Anthem. Our repeated failure to do so led to a cinema closure threat, so we duly complied. There was also a seating dispute. Officers and NCOs sat on chairs paying 7½p, other ranks paying 5p to sit on a backless bench. BORs could not pay the extra 2½p for a chair. Thus began an other ranks cinema boycott accompanied by picketing, but we sooner or later faced the loss of our cinema, so we backed down.

There was an open air cinema for the young ladies of the Women's Army Corps (India) to which we could be invited. Their films were more modern than ours. It was pleasing sitting under the stars in the company of these WAC(I)s, mostly Anglo-Indians, some really pretty. The one snag was showery evenings. One film was never concluded.

Touring companies came occasionally from ENSA (Entertainments National Services Association), but the best was Ralph Reader's No. 13 RAF Gang Show. I had seen Gang Shows at Cardington and Coltishall. These were highly professional and I well remember one comic saying:

'Do you receive your POW parcels regularly?'

This certainly caught the mood of our St Thomas Mount audience.

But service audiences could be cruel. We attended in Madras a concert put on by British civilians. A lady singer was making some extraordinary facial contortions when one of our lads in ringing tones shouted out:

'It's all done by wires!'

It caused a laugh, but was unforgivable.

Whilst temporarily away from St Thomas Mount I missed the chance of seeing a performance of 'Macbeth' in Madras given by a British touring company. At the time, such was my ignorance, that I knew nothing of one of the actors - a chap named John Gielgud!

The most memorable evening was a performance of Handel's 'Messiah' held in the Madras Banqueting Hall. This was a truly magnificent setting with marble pillars and silver chandeliers. The Indian and Anglo-Indian ladies wore silk saris of great beauty. These Indian ladies were of the higher castes only, but even the low-caste Indians performing menial tasks always seemed so graceful with faultless deportment, but the ladies present, including the British, were socially poles apart from poor class Indians.

One evening the Hart Hangar was the venue for a concert principally intended for the Indian airmen. This was excellent entertainment which I thoroughly enjoyed in spite of the language barrier. There was a brilliant group of Chinese acrobats. It was an interesting experience, BORs being warmly invited to attend, which we did - all <u>THREE</u> of us! I am sure half a century on the response would be greater from a similar group of young men. People are now less insular.

Each Saturday evening a music circle was held. A wind-up gramophone was used which played the old type 78 records. We used the tiny information room lit by an oil lamp. Here I was introduced to classical music and really listened for the first time to symphonies, concertos etc. This opened a new musical world. We even had music in the billet. One airman, not always popular, had a set of drums, another, ex-ENSA was an accomplished piano-accordionist.

We sometimes visited the lovely Elliot's Beach, a relaxing spot by the sea. Here we had one of nature's safe drinks, the liquid from an unripened coconut, a watery drink unlike the 'milk' from a ripe coconut.

Football, in spite of the heat and humidity, was popular. I had been in my school football team, but in that climate I was abysmal and gave it up. I was 'running' like a broken-winded horse during the two matches I played. There was a station team, not surprisingly, known as the Saints. In one match the Saints drew 2-2 against the Belfast Regiment who brought along 700 supporters - later our team lost 7-0 to 45 Squadron. The standard of play in those matches was high. How men could achieve it in such a climate was beyond my comprehension.

Also beyond my understanding in those first few weeks was India and Indians. I knew little about the many races, different religions and diverse cultures. To me India was simply part of the vast area of the world that in the atlas was always shaded pink. We used the word empire of which India was a part; it was ours. Yet here I was at nineteen totally perplexed by my new environment, save for the part I understood, namely the RAF.

By and large I had liked most Indians I had met. I respected the personnel of the Royal Indian Air Force with whom I worked. Many had coped with the prejudices of their families before joining the service. Some were Hindus of the highest caste, others Muslims or Sikhs, some were Christians. Their average educational level would have been higher than that of their British counterparts. Some of our BORs thought the Indians less than competent, even lazy. There was no outward hostility though on one awful occasion I heard one RAF airman say to another, in the presence of an IOR:

'The Indians will do anything for a bag of rice'.

This remark though was untypical.

Employed on the aerodrome were many Indians from the lower castes, some the so-called Untouchables. For a mere pittance these people did the menial tasks no-one else would perform such as sweeping, moving rubbish and cleaning the toilets. We had no contact with them. Unlike the IORs most spoke no English.

Most Indian traders in Madras did speak English, but were difficult to deal with, everything being sold by bargaining. The endless haggling over price I disliked, wondering if my 'bargain' was over the top. Far more preferable was to buy from one of the old-established businesses that sold according to a fixed price.

For the Eurasians or Anglo-Indians one could only feel real sympathy. They were the product of relationships usually of British men and Indian women, in some cases generations back. Many were desperate to leave India and 'go home', even though they had as a rule never seen Britain and never would. They knew Indian independence was not too far off. If they decided to stay and most, economically, would have to, would they be welcome? Certainly the Indian railway system seemed heavily dependent upon Anglo-Indian personnel. Ultimately I am sure the majority must have stayed in India.

One of our BORs at St Thomas Mount was engaged to an Anglo-Indian young lady, to the horror of his own parents in the UK. I am sure it worked out for them, but never knew the outcome, our service acquaintances being only fleetingly known.

To increase my understanding of India and Indians I read numerous pamphlets. Initially, like many of my fellow-BORs, I had referred to Indians as 'wogs' ('wily oriental gentlemen'), in my innocence not realising it was a term of contempt. In a few months I was 'converted' and sympathised with Indians in their struggle for independence.

A radio programme a few years ago made the point that soldiers in India pre-World War Two had to supplement their poor rations by buying from vendors. When I was there nothing had changed.

Fruit-wallahs moved from billet to billet selling stubby bananas, small oranges and peanuts in cone-shaped packages made from newspapers. Before buying bananas or oranges we observed that they were correctly dipped in a potassium permanganate solution. This was the medical requirement laid down by the MO.

Char-wallahs at regular intervals called with tea. This was poured from a brass urn fitted with a tap. The lower part of the urn had a charcoal fire so the brew was really strong, too much so for my taste, so I bought only cakes. The most devoted char-wallah I met was one who sat by his urn outside a camp cinema until late in the evening when the programme ended. This in the chill of the Himalayan foothills.

Dhobi-wallahs washed our clothes. These were often taken to a local stream where they were beaten against rounded boulders, the bashing process accompanied by a series of rhythmic grunts. Shirts subjected to this treatment developed frayed collars and cuffs. Drying was usually no problem our laundry being spread out to dry on other boulders or a grassy bank. After pressing, the clothing would normally be returned within 36 hours, the cost being borne by the RAF. However, should we require a speedier return, known as flying dhobi, on payment this could be done in nine hours.

The washing was usually done well and few items were ever lost. The marking system was interesting, dots and dashes. All extremely efficient and much faster than the RAF laundry system in the UK that took ten days.

From time to time traders called selling such items as animals carved from soap stone. On the whole our contact with Indians was fairly limited and almost entirely male.

CHAPTER 18

Demob, Pay and Mail from Home

The possibility of spending four years overseas seemed an eternity of time, but the three years six months for those who were married was infinitely worse. Some of these men had spent years away from wives and children. One airman was so pleased to be going back to his wife and the little three-year-old he had never seen. He showed me the two pairs of shoes he had bought his little lad, but they looked far too small. Poor man, robbed of his child's infancy.

To be tour-ex (tour expired) was one way of going home, but now that the war had ended there was no need for a million-strong RAF and demobilisation began. Each of us was given a demob number based mainly on length of service, though age came into it. The lower one's number the earlier one's demob. Mine was 60, but the vast majority in 1945 would have been groups 20-40. One of our met. staff (Group 25) left for demob. Two non-met. friends, Tom Brabbins and Eric Powell, left for Bombay on 20 December 1945, too late to be home for Christmas. After six years RAF service they deserved to be going home.

By late September '45 it had been announced that the tour for single men was being reduced to three years six months as from December. In my case this would have meant December 1948, but I estimated that I would be demobbed before that anyway. I believed it would be the spring or summer of 1947; an underestimate.

One announcement irritated us. Once we left the forces we were to receive a lump sum known as a gratuity. We understood that in most countries the amounts given related only to length of service, irrespective of rank. Not so in class-conscious Britain where the gratuity was related to service and pay, so those who had already been paid more received more - nothing changes! My gratuity was £35.

As an Aircraftman First Class my basic pay was five shillings and sixpence a day, roughly 26p. On arrival in India this was increased by one shilling a day (5p) Japanese Campaign Pay. This gave me a weekly pay of £2.45, more than adequate for my needs.

At this time in India a haircut cost six annas (3p), two pairs of shorts one rupee (7½p) and a pair of RAF type shoes made by the Indian firm Bata Rs12 (90p).

The Indian currency was based on the rupee (7½p). Three pies equalled one pice, 4 pice equalled one anna and 16 annas made one rupee. The pie was thus worth only .039p which even in those far off days could have bought little.

On 14 September my LAC rank came through and the propellers on each sleeve entitled me to an additional nine pence (4p) each day. I decided to allocate my mother half-a-crown a day (87½p a week) which she drew out and saved for me. It sounds little, but was eventually used as a house deposit.

The receipt of letters was always a great morale booster and I became an inveterate letter writer on the principle that if you don't write them you won't receive them. The mail usually arrived in batches at the beginning of each week. Letters from the UK usually took several days to arrive by air. Newspapers and magazines made the slow sea voyage, but were welcome though outdated. As an example some newspapers posted on the 12 May 1945 did not arrive until 10 July. Reading these British newspapers it was clear that little space had been devoted to the war in the Far East. I now realised just why the 14th Army in Burma had referred to themselves as 'The Forgotten Army'.

My 1945 Christmas present from my parents was a subscription to 'The Manchester Guardian Weekly'. This was printed on incredibly thin paper and came by air mail. I was now better informed of what was happening in the world. In this pre-television era we did not even possess a radio in our billet.

English language papers were published in India, our local one was I believe the 'Madras Mail'. As well as Indian and world news the English language papers reflected the feelings and attitudes of British civilians. One article had suggested that once the war was over British civilians should have repatriation priority over all servicemen. To attain this end it was suggested that the overseas tour for servicemen in India should be extended. It seemed to me that those who had voluntarily come to India pre-1939, thereby missing the Blitz, rationing and other privations, were impertinent to suggest they be allowed to scuttle off at our expense.

One item of news concerned the sentencing of an Indian to six months imprisonment. In a letter to his soldier son serving in Africa he had had the temerity to criticise British rule in India.

Initially all the letters we wrote had, each and every one, to be censored - by officers of course. Naturally we were unable to give any military details or even our whereabouts beyond the bald fact that we were in India. I resented this intrusion into my correspondence. In retrospect I can see that sometimes I wrote deliberate 'digs' for the benefit of my censors as well as my correspondents - criticisms of military discipline, the British ruling class and officers. As far as I know nothing was ever blotted out by the censor. The censorship continued for four weeks after the ending of the war.

Our mail over India was transported by American made Dakotas. Lend-lease over, Dakota spare parts were less available and by January 1946 letters from the UK took three weeks to reach Madras.

CHAPTER 19

October Crashes

Our bashas amongst the trees were not completely waterproof, some were liable to flooding, so they were condemned as unfit to use. We were transferred to the Lawrence Lines which were solidly built ex-army barrack blocks. They were flat-roofed and had massive rooms with high ceilings. Being equipped with electric lighting we found them, being comparatively cool, a big improvement on the bashas. The move, made on 29 September, improved our living conditions considerably.

RAF St. Thomas Mount 1945. L to R: Jack, Ken and Ron.
Background shows typical basha material - interwoven palm.

Being larger meant more occupants which had a drawback. The older men in the basha had been stable and sensible, but they were gradually being replaced by younger arrivals. Once the 'old guard' had gone on demob or tour-ex I found some of the new intake less to my liking. Some were totally intolerant of Indians. There used to be bickering and arguments. One little group did nothing early evening except lie on their backs looking at the ceiling fitfully discussing their two favourite topics - drink and sex, then really late in the evening they would play cards at a time when many of us wished to settle for sleep.

As far as young ladies were concerned the subject was purely academic. Indian women kept their wary distance from us, there were few British girls around and the WAC(I)s in their quarters were separated from us by a high fence, which, as far as I know, none of our lads attempted to climb!

One of the older men I liked and respected left for the UK in October. This was Terry Carnell. He had joined the RAF in 1938 at the age of eighteen. He volunteered for aircrew duties, did 39 operations, mainly over Germany, as an air-gunner. One night he was shot up badly and came off 'ops' in 1942 spending eight months in hospital. No longer able to fly he was reduced in rank from sergeant to corporal and as a final 'reward' sent to India. When I

My second billet at St.Thomas Mount, the Lawrence Lines.
The Mount is in the background.

knew him he suffered a great deal from headaches and at times used to hold onto the side of his bed in fear of falling. He deserved his return home. It was a privilege to have known such men.

On the 24 October I nearly had a close encounter with a Mosquito of the aircraft variety. On take-off a Mosquito hit a stray bullock that had wandered onto the runway. The impact caused the Mosquito to skid off the runway and head towards the Flying Control building in which I was working. The time was 21.15 hrs., it was dark and all I heard was a roar, sufficient to make me realise something was seriously wrong with the aircraft which came to rest about 50 yds (46m) short of our building. Fortunately it did not catch fire and the crew escaped. After a couple of hours the Mosquito, more or less intact, was towed away for repair.

At the time it was happening, my action, walking round our large map table twice, could be considered irrational. I soon calmed down, others were dealing with the accident, my job was to do a weather observation, a 'crash ob' as it was known. What happened to the poor buffalo? No recollection. Our dinner?

Next day another Mosquito crashed on take-off at the end of the main runway. This aircraft was a total 'write-off' - a burnt out wreck. The same day a Liberator transport full of repatriated servicemen also crashed at St Thomas Mount. What happened to the occupants of the two aircraft I cannot recall.

Earlier, on the 12 October I had written:

'Mosquito crashed at the end of the subsidiary runway.'

Four crashes in peacetime on one aerodrome in a fortnight seemed a bit much so I vowed to avoid aeroplane flight where possible.

At this time at St Thomas Mount we had a small unit consisting of a Hurricane and one pilot. The sole duty of the latter being a daily flight to various altitudes to gather meteorological data. Whether he enjoyed this isolation I never got round to asking him.

CHAPTER 20
Hill Party in the Nilgiris

Our leave allowance was one month each year, but in addition every few months we joined what was known as a hill party. This meant a short stay in one of the hill stations, our nearest being the Nilgiris. Hastings Holiday Home, Wellington was a military camp open to army, navy or air force personnel.

My first hill party was 15-29 November 1945. We travelled by train from Madras to Mettupalaiyam. The rest of the journey was normally made on a narrow gauge rack rail system, but when we arrived the Nilgiri Mountain Railway was out of action (landslide). Instead we travelled the 20 miles to Wellington in a naval transport. The driver was a good one, fortunately, since the road had hairpin bends and many sheer drops. At one point an Indian workman, for reasons unknown, dropped a boulder in front of the lorry.

The camp was 6,000 ft. above sea level (1,848m) It was in cloud when we arrived, cool and damp. The billets were comfortable, the food reasonable; we soon felt at home.

Wellington had two cinemas and a number of service clubs. The main Nilgiri town was Ootacamund, known to all as 'Ooty'. I made three visits to Ooty which had a lake and some interesting bookshops. On one occasion, some of us travelled by rail. The little Swiss-built locomotive pushed its four coaches at 15 m.p.h. The rack system was employed, in places dealing with a 1:15 gradient. The scenery was wonderful - valleys and terraced hills on which tea was grown, beautiful wooded hills and waterfalls.

The fortnight's break was refreshing. We wore what we liked and did as we pleased. The scenery, when the cloud cleared that is, was lovely and it was real joy to snuggle under blankets during the chilly nights.

One evening we enjoyed an ENSA concert, there were films to see, books to read and some superb walks. On one occasion some of us visited Coonoor;

once Kotagiri. Both these little places, like Ooty, by virtue of altitude enjoyed a European-type climate. This was what attracted British tea planters, army officers and administrators who happily settled with their wives; ideal places for retirement. Kotagiri I found very like England, the whites being friendlier than those in Madras. It was in Kotagiri that I met a pleasant English girl in the Toc H. This may seem unremarkable, but there were few opportunities of meeting young women in India. I even discovered a delightful reading room which had easy chairs and a real log fire.

On the 28 November, our last day, we were shown round a tea plantation, a retired doctor being our guide. The estate consisted of 400 acres (162 hectares) of tea with also a little coffee. The tea bushes grew to a height of 3 to 4 ft. (0.9 - 1.2m). Only the tips of the leaves were plucked, this being done every ten days by coolies, as the women pickers were called. The tea, after the drying process, was rolled and sieved on large moving trays of varying mesh. Some of the tea was thrown by the machinery onto the floor, being swept up by ladies using hand brushes. Asked what happened to the sweepings we were told that much of it would be sold to military camps! Sorry we asked.

Nilgiri Mountain Railway 1:16 gradient

Men employed in the factory were paid one rupee a day (7½p), women earning 5p and children 2p. Evidently many of the women and children contracted tuberculosis. This seemed to be accepted as quite normal.

So ended a wonderful two weeks. Next day it was back to reality. As we descended from Wellington it grew steadily hotter and we shed clothes. At Mettupalaiyam we waited four hours for the Madras-bound troop train, beggars and vendors at every station. At one, Arkonam, a sweet little Indian girl earned money by singing in English songs made famous by Deanna Durbin the film star. I have a remembrance of 'Red Sails in the Sunset'.

The journey was fairly comfortable having the luxury of leather seats and not the usual hard wooden type.

During the winter 'cool' season life became more bearable, but even so the maximum by day usually reached at least 80°F (27°C) and the minimum at night would seldom fall below 70°F (21°C). Just occasionally it dropped to 60°-65°.

It was during this cooler spell that on 1 December I was lucky enough to be included in a party one of the officers had organised to visit two historic sights revered by Hindus. Fifteen of us travelled by lorry a round trip of 106

Hastings Holiday Home, Wellington, Nilgiri Hills, 1945.
A hill station used by British soldiers, sailors and airmen.

miles, taking a supply of K-rations and water with us. Initially the road was good,, but eventually petered out to become a rough trackway. The journey was through countryside so typical of southern India - ricefields and avenues of coconut palms.

Our first stop was Tirukallikundram, a Shiva temple built on top of a rocky site known as Vadigari Hill. The temple was reached in my reckoning by 400 steps (a modern guide says 565). Earlier we had been given flowers which we placed on a stone at the peak, where we met the usual crowd of beggars asking for baksheesh.

We were there at 10.30 too early to see the two white Egyptian vultures that arrived each day at noon. They were said to be reincarnated saints on a journey from Benares (now Varanasi) to Rameshwaram. The vultures had a good daily meal from the hands of one of the priests, but the journey of 800 mls (1,287km) was highly improbable.

From Tirukallikundram we travelled to Mahabalipuram, where between AD610-640 some superb Hindu temples and other sacred buildings had been hewn from solid rock which must have been a vast undertaking.

The site was near the seashore and some buildings were already engulfed by the sea. Although we had little idea of the religious significance of the carved buildings and animals they were impressive under the sunlight in that coastal setting. The site was known as the Seven Pagodas. The buildings had been completed during the reign of Mamalla, one of the Pallava kings who ruled a considerable portion of southern India from AD300-800.

The Siva temple on Vadigari Hill, Tirukallikundram.
The Egyptian Vulture wheeling at the top arrives for a daily meal.

The Seven Pagodas Mahabalipuram. Some parts of this beautiful site
are crumbling into the Bay of Bengal.

CHAPTER 21
'Ma' Weston and Kotagiri

During the 1945-46 winter the monsoon 'failed' in the sense that the north-easterly winds brought less rain than expected. This left the area short of rice. We feared a repetition of the disastrous Bengal famine of 1943 which the older airmen told us about. Deaths during the famine were conservatively put at three-quarters of a million.

It had been rumoured that half the personnel of 743 FC would be posted to Ceylon, but it did not happen and surprisingly only seven weeks after leaving the lovely Nilgiri Hills I was back again. Ideally it would have been better to have taken leave during the hot season thereby escaping from the heat. But as far as leave was concerned once your turn came you took it.

On the 15 January I left Madras spending my leave at Kotagiri. The train journey was much as usual, being peered at as curiosities each time the train stopped - little faces glued to the carriage windows; then there were the char-wallahs offering us tea in the small hours. After changing trains it was up the mountain railway.

We were to stay with a Eurasian lady known to all as 'Ma' Weston. She had four grown-up children of her own, long since flown, and gave holidays to up to a dozen servicemen at a time. She was a wonderful lady who gave us a marvellous break at 'Athol Brae'. This lady deserved a decoration for all that she did for BORs.

Around 150 British families lived in Kotagiri, planters, wives of serving officers and so on. They lived in large scattered houses employing Indian servants. We were told that only six residents had ever been known to entertain British servicemen. Would we have been on that same wavelength and did they realise this?

On the 18th we walked the four miles to a beautiful spot, Elk Falls. On nearing the falls we helped ourselves to three haversacks of fruit from a nearby tangerine grove. This in reality was blatant theft had we thought it through. They were not growing wild and on scrambling the 30m to the bottom of the falls we were stoned by Indians. One of our lads was hit on the shoulder so we armed ourselves with sticks before making the return journey, thinking we might be attacked. When we arrived at the village the children greeted us by singing the National Anthem. I still feel totally ashamed of this episode, robbing these poor people.

The weather was fickle. We had two damp, misty days when we were unable to leave the house. When we did venture out we climbed to the top of Dimhatti Betta which was 7,000 ft (2,134m) above sea level. The view was superb. To the north was the Mysore Plateau, to east and west the Nilgiris, to the south the plains and a range of hills 50 miles away. The 'climb' was virtually a stiff trek, but breathing came heavily because of exercising at altitude - and the fact that some of us were not fit!

Next day we climbed Dodda Betta (8,640 ft. a.s.l. = 2,633m) the Nilgiris highest spot. We had taken a bus, then walked two miles. At the summit was a ruined meteorological observatory. From this spot there was a view of 75 miles in some directions, mainly a tree-covered landscape. Descending we did a four mile walk to Ootacamund.

A Todha elder in the Nilgiri Hills.

That day some of us met Mr Nooney, a strange man who invited a few of us to his home. He looked Indian, had a house full of eastern-style carpets and silks. His house contained an American radio, many English books, and the bearded mystery man who disliked Indians, played the saxophone. With Mr Nooney we occasionally played Mah Jhong. Poor man, one evening he asked our party, which included an Irish sailor, whether we would like to come round to hear him play the saxophone. 'Yes' said 'Paddy' - 'on Thursday'.

'Why Thursday?' asked Mr Nooney stroking his beard as usual. *'Because I leave on Wednesday!'* - Paddy replied ungraciously.

On 25 January we 'cycled' to Kodanaad, ten miles away, though because of the hills we walked three miles of it. On route we passed a Todha settlement. This remote group of people were clearly dying out because of tuberculosis, but now things look brighter for them. The Todhas relied upon cattle for their livelihood. The men had long flowing beards and looked for all the world like Biblical figures - Abraham and his sons come to life.

At Kodanaad there was a large tea plantation, but the weather had been dry for some days and insufficient tea could be picked to keep the factory working.

From the highest part of the plantation the view was magnificent. Between the Nilgiris and the Mysore Plateau lay 'The Ditch'. This was a valley many miles wide and at that time the home of elephants, wild boar, tigers and leopards. The area looked inhospitable and bleak and was a hunting ground for rajahs; not a place to be alone on a dark night.

Two days later we again hired cycles and headed for Coonoor to have a last look around. At one spot on the journey from the top of a rock we looked down on the mountain railway 2,000 ft. below. It looked for all the world like a minute caterpillar crawling along a cotton thread. Opposite the rock was a Drug or fort. According to 'Ma' Weston Indian soldiers had once been in the habit of throwing enemies over the nearby precipice. Typically brave I stayed well away from the edge.

Next day one of our party had a twenty-first birthday celebration attended by twelve BORs and a similar number of locals. One was a colonel in 'civvies', a sociable pleasant man, unlike two officers' wives who were showing off. It was an excruciating evening consisting of embarrassing party games and dancing which in those days was formal and it was necessary to know the steps, an art unfamiliar to Ken and me. We felt like social outcasts. A good time was had by all - except for two!

So ended the holiday, a memorable experience, made so interesting by our hostess. Yet curiously enough in a way I was glad to be returning to 'normal' life at St Thomas Mount. But I would miss those wonderful meals, the scenery and the cool climate.

CHAPTER 22
The RAF India Mutiny 1946

Towards the end of my Kotagiri leave it came as a surprise to hear that thousands of my fellow airmen in India were on strike. There was of course a widespread feeling of disgruntlement, but this was an unprecedented step. Under RAF regulations the very word strike was a misnomer; the RAF recognised only mutiny.

As early as November 1945 some 2,000 airmen at the large base of Jodhpur had stopped working. The authorities called in Indian troops. But the main period of the strike was during the latter half of January 1946, triggered off by events at Drigh Road, Karachi. News of the action was spread around by means of wireless-telegraphy. If unable to use wireless operators, messages were chalked on the fuselages of departing aeroplanes urging other aerodromes to join in. Dum Dum, Cawnpore, Mauripur, Vizagapatam and over fifty other units followed suit, involving a massive number of airmen, some estimates being 50,000. At its peak around forty per cent of India's RAF airmen were mutineers having downed tools and disobeyed their officers.

The strike had now spread to Singapore where on 26 January at Seletar another large force of 4,000 airmen took part. This RAF India affair had produced the biggest ever military insurrection in British history.

The strike was an angry spontaneous defiance aimed at the Government as well as the RAF. On the organisational side airmen who were members of both Labour and Communist parties played a prominent part, as undoubtedly did trade unionists. These men were activists, which is not to say that the strikers were politically motivated.

Why did it happen? The main reason was the slow rate of demobilisation. The bulk of RAF personnel consisted of civilians who had either volunteered or been conscripted. These men had shared a common wartime purpose, namely to defeat Nazi Germany and its allies. They had regarded it as a just war and with hostilities now at an end wished only to return to civilian life. But the Government, a Labour one at that, had a vast empire to maintain and keep in order. To this aim Labour had a plan deciding it was easier and cheaper to police the Far East from the air than on land. In consequence RAF demob lagged behind that of the Army and even more of the Royal Navy. Our lads felt betrayed from a quarter where it had been unexpected.

'Operation Python' the codename for the demobilisation of RAF personnel in South-East Asia, was way behind target. This was aggravated by an acute shipping shortage brought about by the massive tonnage sunk by U-boats. Long-range aircraft were not available in any realistic quantity. For the two months before the January strike demob had been almost at a standstill.

There were other causes. There was a deep social divide between the officers and the other ranks. Officers had superior living conditions and this was harder to bear in such a harsh climate. Also RAF airmen served as cheap labour for the British Overseas Airways Corporation, servicing their airliners. This also applied to Indian civil airlines. The attitude was why should we? Part of our met. work was in the civilian category.

The strike/mutiny spread over a fortnight or so and caused embarrassment to Air Chief Marshall Sir Keith Park, commanding the RAF in South East Asia. His instructions from London gave authority to use the Army if necessary. The RAF and the Government were both in a quandary.

What impact the strike had on the folks back home I never did discover, but perhaps they knew little about it. Were they ever told the facts, even we only heard in dribs and drabs. But on the journey from Kotagiri to St Thomas Mount I had made up my mind to join the strikers. There was, however, no question of doing so since our St Thomas Mount airmen had not participated and by the time I was back the strike had fizzled out all over India.

An enquiry was held and numerous airmen were questioned by the Special Investigation Branch of the RAF. Their task was to find the ringleaders so they could be punished. As a Conservative MP had said whilst in India:

'The men must be crushed'.

The strike had a number of positive effects. Demob speeded up, information about release became more accessible and detailed, lists being pinned up showing troopships leaving Bombay. The RAF did a better public relations job. Men were going home in greater numbers, somehow ships were found. But the strike failed to achieve any improvement in our living conditions.

In retrospect, one can see the fears of the authorities. Indian independence had not yet been agreed and the last thing they wanted were disaffected British and Indian military personnel, should Indians stage a widespread rebellion against the British. One consequence of the RAF strike may have been the actions of Indian sailors in what became known as the Royal Indian Navy Mutiny. Did the RAF give the RIN an example to follow?

CHAPTER 23
The Royal Indian Navy Mutiny

Once the war ended we became virtually an army of occupation. As individuals we were treated with friendliness, though collectively we were not wanted - certainly by the more nationalist Indians who desired freedom from British rule. For many Indians, such as our bearer, there must have been mixed feelings since we represented their livelihood. Certainly in Madras I was treated with courtesy and met no animosity, though that may have depended upon one's own attitude.

Whilst I was on leave Mahatma Gandhi spoke in Madras city on 23 January. It would have been great to have seen him, but to our airmen the city was out of bounds that day. Incidents were occurring, as when an Indian made as if to throw himself under an RAF lorry. Fortunately the driver stopped. To have run over the civilian could have led to a lynching. Indians, normally quiet people, were volatile in a large crowd. Generally there was no violence directed against British forces. It was usually verbal, telling our lads to 'Quit India' - sentiments with which all of us agreed. They wished us out, we had no desire to stay.

By mid-February there was trouble in Calcutta, the seat of more civil disobedience than Madras. Bengalis were more politically conscious than Madrassis and one bone of contention was the former Indian National Army. These were Indians who, under their leader Subhas Chandra Bose, had defected to the Japanese cause. Some had been condemned to death, but a public outcry led to their release. In Calcutta nineteen US soldiers were injured, but had no authority to retaliate.

Madras joined in the civil disobedience campaign, transport workers striking. Students at the university issued a proclamation decrying the shooting by police in Calcutta of allegedly peacefully protesting citizens.

More seriously, on 20 February the Royal Indian Navy was on strike, in

Bombay initially, the insurrection spreading to Karachi and Calcutta. Dozens of RIN ships were involved and 20,000 sailors; the initial trigger being abusive racist language by British officers.

On the 21st some of our Saint Thomas Mount Mosquitos left for Santa Cruz, a Bombay area airfield much nearer the action. They left armed with bombs, rockets and cannon shells. Sixteen other St Thomas Mount Mosquitos soon followed.

The RIN had seized the 'Hindustan' which fired on Karachi. In Bombay there was fighting between British and Indians. The US Embassy was attacked, the Stars and Stripes being torn down and burnt. The city was the scene of widespread riots, looting and killing. Over 200 Indians were killed and hundreds injured. It was deemed unsafe for British servicemen, so troopships stopped sailing and demob was held up. Meanwhile, on 22 February, the IORs at St Thomas Mount staged a short-lived two hour strike.

Next day a Dakota of No. 10 Squadron took off from our aerodrome carrying a cargo of rockets. The same day I spent much of my time reading 'Emma'. Essential reading was not to be held up by mutinies or strikes!

By the 25th the Indian Naval Mutiny was over so our Mosquitos came 'home', first 82 Squadron, then No. 45. Actually neither squadron had been able to operate at full strength. Some of the Mosquitos had warped wings due to the heat and sun. Wood of course played an important part in the structure of a Mosquito.

Although disturbances at Bombay and Karachi were almost at a standstill it was not so in Madras, where on 26 February there was much rioting. Some BORs were stoned and an ambulance set on fire. Transport and electricity workers had downed tools. Demonstrations were taking place. I had decided, not too wisely, to visit Madras, but at the Guardroom they told me to turn back.

During the next day or so shops with European names were attacked, as well as cinemas and Chinese restaurants. No British lives were lost, though some BORs were attacked at the railway station. At Saidapet, four miles from St Thomas Mount, Indians were sprawling across the railway tracks to stop all train movements. One RAF despatch rider on his motor-cycle found himself in a tight spot surrounded by agitators. Firing his revolver above his head enabled him to escape.

Some strange tales did the rounds. One was that marching protesters in Bombay had been joined by British servicemen who joined in the chanting of

'Jai Hind' (Long Live India).

At this time I was disturbed to realise what should have been obvious, namely, that the aerodrome was a possible target for agitators. A defence plan had been drawn up and the Station Armoury contained sten guns and other weapons. We had all had instruction in the use of firearms and could be used in aerodrome defence. What would I do? In theory, I would obey orders, fire over heads, or whatever told to do. Luckily I had no such choice to make, for which I was glad.

On the night 26/27 February around 200 rioters did break into the aerodrome intent on arson. The station police dealt with the Indians before they could burn down too many bashas. Our help was not needed - thankfully. What the Indian airmen thought of it I don't know. By a touch of irony, it was their billets, and not the British, that were burnt.

By early March Madras was again peaceful. When I did resume my visits it was with a wary sense of unease, though with familiarity this soon passed.

CHAPTER 24

Never Volunteer - It Could Be Borneo!

Thirteen new personnel arrived at 743 FC in October 1945, some wireless-operators, but mostly met. assistants. We were clearly overstaffed. Four of us volunteered to be posted elsewhere. Our CO said he could not lose four of his most experienced airmen and decided on two only. We tossed a coin for it and I lost, thereby staying at St Thomas Mount. I had a hunch that it might well have been to Japan where the maximum temperature would not have been 90-100°+ for most of the year and there would have been a different culture to experience. Actually it was Borneo and only one man was needed.

Whilst I was on leave at Kotagiri two others were sent, so had I not been in the Nilgiris I might well have been one of them. From one of the three I received a letter saying he was on Labuan Island, off the cost of Borneo. The climate was hot and wet, they lived in tents, their sole water supply was the rain and the food was entirely tinned. I realised what I had escaped, decided to sit tight and count my blessings. What had the old hands always told us? Never volunteer!

Three from 743 FC applied for commissions in the RAF Regiment, two being successful. Four totally inexperienced Indians arrived, all needing to be trained. This happened several times. We always seemed overstaffed and by the end of '45 we worked only thirty hours a week and after a night duty were allowed a sleeping day followed by a free day. All dead easy and better than Labuan.

Had I not been sent to India I would later have gone to Germany, all UK male met. assistants were being sent there at this time. Germany was a country that fascinated me and I was green with envy!

Although demob was far off, my thoughts turned to my post-RAF life. Staying in the RAF was not an option, all met. assistants were to be civilians as now. The civilian Met. Office was a possibility, I enjoyed the work. My pre-RAF employers, Barclays Bank, would have to offer me my old job back, but I detested office life, so that was out. University was only possible if I could take 'A' levels. Teaching was also a possibility since I liked the idea of work of a social nature, perhaps with children. I wrote at the time:

> *'When I am an old man I want to look back on life and see*
> *a little good I have done'.*

I hope my balance sheet is on the credit side.

Most RAF stations had an Education Section with an officer in charge. At St Thomas Mount it took me several days to locate it, tucked away in an odd corner of the airfield. It had a good library and plenty of career leaflets and details of the Ministry of Labour's Emergency Teacher Training Course. I applied for this one year course, but only those twenty-one or over could be accepted and I was only twenty.

The RAF introduced Educational and Vocational Training (EVT for short). This began in March 1946. At Coltishall via the Education Section I took a correspondence course in geography so decided to give EVT a go. We did nine hours each week, my subjects being English, maths, geography, economics and world affairs.

One of our instructors was a Jew. So far I had known six Jewish airmen and they compared favourably with the rest, being intelligent, well-educated and politically progressive. My one reservation was the Jew who had stolen my life-jacket on the 'Chitral'. At this time there were some forty Jewish Labour MPs. But this is to digress. As far as EVT was concerned it was both useful and interesting.

One Sunday morning, 24 March, towards the end of my time at St Thomas Mount, being at a loose end, I wandered the airfield and came across the Salvage Section which for someone keen on aircraft recognition was a 'plane spotter's paradise. Here I found a Stirling, a Wellington and a Liberator. All three were minus engines, but complete in all other respects including the pilots' control columns. Externally so sleek and streamlined, internally they were a confusing mass of wiring, cables and equipment.

The Wellington in particular fascinated me. During the early years of the war many had been based at RAF Marham and often flew over my hometown, Swaffham.

On the night 7/8 July 1941 a Wellington of 75 Squadron based at Mildenhall, had been attacked by a German night fighter, following a raid on

Münster. Sergeant J A Ward, the co-pilot, noticed the starboard wing on fire near the engine. He clambered out of the perspex astrodome on top of the fuselage, kicked hand and footholds in the canvas covering of the geodetic framework of the wing. Desperately holding on, to avoid being plucked into eternity by the slipstream, he beat out the flames enabling his 'plane to reach the UK. For his bravery Sgt. Ward was awarded the Victoria Cross, but was killed two months later.

I was well aware of the young New Zealander's tremendous courage as I re-enacted the above, squeezing through the astrodome, kicking footholds and so forth. Easy enough at ground level, but how about two or three miles up? The morning increased my respect for the men of Bomber Command. The latter have to my mind been denigrated by some historians in recent years, which is easy with hindsight. The massive destruction of so many German cities can only be viewed with misgivings, but this is only part of the story. The RAF and USAAF raids disrupted German industry and transport. By the end of 1943 two-thirds of all Luftwaffe fighters were being used for the defence of the Third Reich, fighters which could have been used against the Russians bearing the brunt of land fighting. The young men of Bomber Command deserve our respect not condemnation.

CHAPTER 25
The Good Life - For Nine Days

In early 1946 it was clear that meteorology personnel were lagging behind in demob. Anyone who did reach Bombay could wait some weeks for a troopship. BORs in met. were five groups behind most other trades, though one of our men did have an early demob under Class B release because in civilian life he had been a plumber.

In March it was announced that six months was being knocked off the tour for a single man. Good news indeed, down to three years, of which I had done nearly a year.

Mid-tour leave was to begin. To be eligible one had to have been overseas for at least twelve months and also be at least eighteen demob groups ahead of current release. The leave was designed to give three weeks in the UK. Initially it was an air journey home and a troopship return, later to be ship both ways. Lots had to be drawn, but I have no remembrance of it. Hundreds applied from our 225 Group in May, me included, but only twenty were successful. I knew only one 'winner'.

29 Group Met. Assistants were demobbed in February '46, Group 45 in September '46. Mine I estimated as February 1947. Not a chance!

In March I was on a 'good scrounge' - a week's fire duty for which we were excused all normal duties and parades. The fire picket was from 17.30 hrs.-08.00 hrs. At 20.00 the fire tender took us to the cinema, admission free, supper following, then a night's sleep. Next day was ours until 17.30. All a bit farcical since we had had no fire training to deal with an emergency.

Another 'scrounge' was the Dramatic Arts course at Bangalore. The latter had a cooler climate than Madras, so two of us put our names down. Only one could go, but neither fancied it alone.

About this time we heard that all our met. officers in India were being posted to the UK. What would happen to us? Would we be officerless, have

Indian forecasters or be sent further east e.g. Malaya. One thing was for sure - <u>we</u> would not be going home en masse!

Towards the end of March a new CO arrived, a New Zealander. He was genuinely interested in the welfare of other ranks and was immediately labelled a good type. One of his first acts was to do an inspection of our billets, meet us informally, and give us a chance to freely air our grievances. We spoke frankly telling him amongst other things that the food was 'deadly.'

On 25 March he called together all the officers and gave them a stern lecture, the beginning of a number of brushes with his fellow officers. Our 'good type' in their eyes was a tyrant. At the first meeting he told the officers they knew nothing of the living conditions of BORs and IORs. One officer was asked if he ever inspected the airmen's billets. The poor man knew nothing of his men's living-quarters and was told to:

'B_____ well find out.'

The CO pointed out that unless certain officers pulled their socks up they would be losing rank. The Airmen's Mess he rightly described as a hole, to which he would not take his worst enemy, for a meal.

Within days the CO cancelled the colour-hoisting parades making it abundantly clear that he had no time for 'bull', which he regarded as ridiculous and pointless.

On 3 April an awesome sight awaited us in the Airmen's Mess. The food was actually piled on plates for us to help ourselves. There was celery stuffed with cheese, spring onions, tomatoes, cucumber, spam, corned beef, biscuits and iced coffee made with milk. The CO had told the Catering Officer if he needed food for the airmen to take money from the fund of the Officers' Mess. The officers by now must have concluded that their tyrant was a plundering villain!

On 7 April we had another building in use as our Airmen's Mess. Why had the building not been used before? In fact need the food have been so mediocre for the previous months? When we entered our restaurant-type mess we were astonished to find the old chipped enamelled plates no longer needed. We were eating from china and the tables had - tablecloths! There was even a machine for the making of ice-cream. All ice had previously gone to the Officers' Mess.

By any standard things were looking good at 'Tommy's Bump' and as a final icing on the cake all parades were forthwith cancelled. All was well, we were on to a good thing, then to my utter annoyance, two days later, I found

I was being sent on detachment to Vizagapatam. Footballers go on loan to other clubs, RAF personnel on loan were 'detached'.

Now Vizagapatam was an isolated aerodrome on the coast of the Bay of Bengal midway between Calcutta and Madras. It enjoyed a poor reputation with a climate allegedly worse than that of St Thomas Mount, plus poor living conditions. I had stuck St Thomas Mount for ten months when it was often grim, now that it had immeasurably improved I was posted. I cursed my bad luck, leaving when things were so good.

Anyway I liked being near Madras. It was an interesting city with a history closely associated with the East India Company which established a fort and factory there in 1639. Fort St George, with its association with Robert Clive, I visited in my early days at St Thomas Mount. A guide showed one room in which Clive allegedly attempted to commit suicide, but failed. Later his words were:

'I feel that I am reserved for some end or other'.

He was and helped found British rule in India.

Nearby was the lighthouse from which one gained a marvellous view of the city for which I have always reserved a soft spot.

CHAPTER 26
First Thoughts on Vizagapatam

10 April was to be my last day at St Thomas Mount. Although only on detachment to Vizagapatam the move was made permanent four days later.

The heat at this time was horribly unpleasant, we sweated profusely and clothes became soaked. This led to more prickly heat, especially tormenting at night times, with the intense burning and pricking.

The next day I left Madras on the 480 miles (772km) journey, travelling on the Calcutta troop train which meant only a limited number of stops, just to drop off servicemen. Even so our average speed was only 19 mph (30.6 km/h). With so few stops I slept until 05.00, unusual on an Indian train journey.

There was a dining car which allegedly would prepare meals - principally dried biscuits! To be fair we did once have jacket potatoes, but mainly filled up with tinned herring and corned beef.

Near Rajahmundry we crossed the 9,096 ft. (2,772m) bridge over the river Godavari, at this season a mere trickle of water in the middle of a dry, sandy river bed. Children always seemed to be waiting for passing trains. We threw down some of the hard RAF biscuits which, in spite of the height of the bridge, hit the river bed without breaking. To see the Godavari on a map of India reminds me of gliding biscuits.

Vizagapatam, shown on modern maps as Vishakapatnam, was a port on the Bay of Bengal. The airfield was two or three miles from the sea and our living quarters two miles away. The airfield itself was surrounded by hills except on the seaward side. Our billets, cookhouse, Station Sick Quarters, cinema and administration buildings lay beneath the Kailasa Hills.

Vizag pronounced 'Vi' to rhyme with 'eye' and 'zag' (to rhyme with 'bag') was just a staging post for 'planes to stop and refuel. Two transport Dakotas arrived each day, one going north, one south. They carried a few passengers, but the one from Madras to Calcutta brought our eagerly awaited mail, a morale-booster in such an isolated spot.

The billets were the usual bashas, but better than those at St Thomas Mount. We were told that they had once been occupied by the US Army Air Force. The Americans normally cared more for the welfare of their other ranks than the British did. The huts were made of the customary wood and

My home at Vizag for ten months - Basha B5. What happened to it?

RAF Vizagapatam. Airmen's basha amongst the palm trees.
Kailasa Hills in the background.

thatch, but had solid concrete floors and the roofs had a metal lining.

The airfield was quiet, desolate and lonely as a workplace. It had only four resident aircraft - an Auster, two Vengeances and a Tiger Moth, all hopelessly unserviceable. Eventually only the Tiger Moth remained, a forlorn sight being slowly consumed by termites and other aeroplane nibblers.

On 15 April I wrote:

> *'The aerodrome is practically deserted and there is a deathly silence about the place, disturbed only by an occasional train whistle from the locomotives which run between the 'drome and our billets. It is for all the world as if we have been left to spend the rest of our lives in this desolate spot amongst the palm trees and hills. The really astonishing part of it is that it isn't a dream, but is really happening in 1946.'*

To reach the aerodrome we travelled by RAF lorry, if this broke down, not unknown, we walked over the railway line and then amongst the tiny fields where the villagers were at work.

Life at Vizag was wonderfully informal. There were no parades, no colour-hoisting ceremonies, not even pay parades. When we collected our pay we simply called in Pay Accounts and had a word with the officer.

We virtually wore what we liked and that was little, often only shorts, socks and sandals. Everyone was really laid back and we even walked into the cookhouse in the same state of undress.

At the airfield Vazagapatam. Our only resident aeroplane - a 'Tiger Moth'.

Vizag was hot and incredibly damp. To not have a wet, perspiring body was almost impossible. At night even the sheets and pillows soon became damp. We frequently took a cold shower, dried ourselves, liberally applied talcum powder, but by the time we had walked the couple of minutes back to the basha we would be wet once more.

For health reasons the maximum time to be spent at this outpost of the British Empire was twelve months. After this the reward was a posting, if possible, to somewhere cooler, usually Yelahanka, near Bangalore.

During the first few days of my stay there were several heavy showers, unusual in April. The storms were often violent, rushing currents of air and torrential rain. At least it was a break from the everlasting, searing sun. After these downpours the numerous dry gullies between our billets became incredible mini-torrents. Occasionally we stood outside naked, joyfully letting the rain pour down our hot bodies. The bullfrogs too enjoyed all the rain and croaked their delight. This was a characteristic Vizag sound.

By late April I had prickly heat on my back, stomach and rear quarters. It looked like measles, really hurt, but there was little chance of it going before October. To make up for the loss of salt due to this excessive perspiring many of us took salt tablets. The body found it difficult to cope with this dampness.

On 3 May 1946 732 FC consisted of an officer, of whom I remember nothing and seven airmen in all. John Buckenham, the corporal, at 21, was the senior airman. He was the one who had 'got some service in' and had been in Burma. This had toughened him up and he spoke his mind. He had two passions, socialism and classical music. Iain Malcolm from Middlesex, because of his Scottish origins, was known to all as 'Mac'. He spent much of his spare time studying French and Latin. On demob he would go to Pembroke College, Cambridge. 'Mac', unlike me, knew where he was going and

Jack waiting for transport to Vizagapatam's airfield, 1946.

113

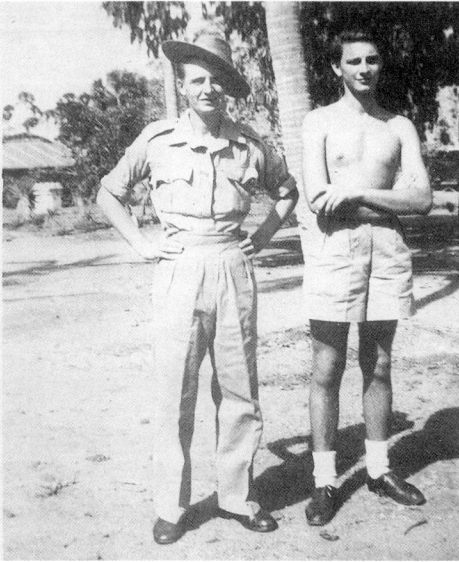

RAF Vizagapatam July 1946 'Mac' (Iain) with bush hat at a jaunty angle, author in preferred 'uniform'.

'Jock' Elliot at Vizagapatam.

why. He was a sincere Christian always playing himself down, but he was a fine person for whom I had the utmost respect. Together we shared all our hopes and fears. For years we remained friends until his death. Like John, 'Mac' was also a corporal.

William, 'Jock' Elliot from a village near Berwick-on-Tweed was a heavily built easy-going Scot. His father had a smallholding and 'Jock', as we all did, longed for his own environment. 'Jock' was a good friend to us all, a generous-hearted pleasant man, tortured by prickly heat. Sadly, he died prematurely of a heart attack in 1989 and poor 'Mac' four years later.

Dennis Foster had been posted with me from St Thomas Mount and was a quiet, friendly, likeable lad who I was also with when I eventually left Vizag.

The mystery man of the bunch was Johnnie Costello allegedly from Jersey City, USA. We always felt he was Anglo-Indian. He was the only married man and had a most beautiful wife with dark eyes and black hair. They had a two-month-old baby, equally attractive.

Today I believe Vishakapatnam (Vizag's present name) is India's fourth largest port with a population of one million. Its 1942 population was only 75,000. At that time the Japanese had bombed it, though most of the inhabitants had been evacuated.

I made my first visit on 24 April writing:

> *'It consists of one long street which has open sewers down one side. The town contains a few scruffy-looking shops, no English cinemas and one forces canteen which is actually run for the Merchant Navy and contains only four tables.*
>
> *I saw dozens of lepers and deformed beggars. Vizag looks a dirty, stinking hole. May I leave this country soon.'*

Unfair, perhaps a snap judgement, but that was my impression.

On 7 May:

> *'Night duty. Later paid my second visit to Vizagapatam. The town stank as before with its gutters full of dead vegetation, dirty water, paper and plain excreta. The smell is awful, but these Indian towns are fascinating though I am often the only European in sight.*
>
> *Coming back I managed a lift, but got mixed up in my bearings and landed up on a rough track, with the aerodrome three miles away. Walked a bit, then crossed onto the railway track for a couple of miles until a train came along, a goods hurtling towards Calcutta. Eventually arrived at camp feeling hot and tired.'*

Vizag town was like most of India, full of beggars. They were on the streets, on railway stations - some blind, others gruesomely deformed. Many were incredibly young, others pathetically old. They sat on the pavements with pleading eyes and outstretched hands. Some followed us, but to give to one was only to increase the number. It was hard to ignore them, hard to shake them off. Like every other young BOR I never discovered how to deal with the poor beggars with that interminable cry of 'baksheesh'. No wonder the word buckshee entered the English language. Little did I think that half a century later we would see the same pathetic bundles of society's rejects huddled in English doorways.

CHAPTER 27
Food - or the lack of

On 27 April we had a VIP visitor, Sir Archibald Nye, who arrived in the inevitable Dakota. The local police lined the runway, splendid in their green and red uniforms. Some of these poor policemen had been standing some hours in the blazing sun, some had arrived the previous day. Pomp and ceremony abounded in India.

Our lads carried on with their work unconcerned by the Governor and his entourage. We worked in customary fashion with shirts off, socks around the ankles and with unavoidably dusty shoes. The sequel to our devil-may-care slovenliness came a month later. Station Orders mentioned that 225 Group HQ was not all pleased with Vizag's airmen owing to the general standard of 'untidiness, lack of discipline' etc. It gave us a laugh to read that 'the practice of wearing socks around the ankles is to be deplored'.

To walk around and work as we did was cooler, but looking back I believe it was a form of passive resistance allied to awkwardness, as was the practice of not saluting officers. We resented the difference in their standard of living and ours. Our pay was much less, our quarters inferior, the food poorer. They knew the luxury of ceiling fans and electric lighting.

The Governor paid a further visit on 19 July and again on 13 December 1946, on which occasion I wrote:

> *"The Governor of Madras, Sir Archibald Nye, is visiting us today, or should I say his 'plane is landing here, the first 'plane we've had here for weeks. By the preparations made on the aerodrome one would think that the King was coming. Flying Control has been whitewashed and even the inside of lavatories. I don't think he will take the slightest notice anyway. I wish he could wander around by himself asking questions about our living conditions, then we could tell him a thing or two.'*

After one visit by the Governor a local paper reported:

> 'His Excellency was accosted by a resident of the adjoining village of Ariyakudi. The villager complained that the place was not provided with protected water, medical and educational facilities and children had to walk four miles to attend a school, carrying their tiffin with them.'

The Governor remarked:

> *'When I was a boy I walked five miles to attend a school, carrying my tiffin with me, and that is why I am strong - walking will certainly do much good to boys.'*

The Governor asked him to get rid of his pessimism and smile. The villager smiled broadly, arousing the remark 'That is it, keep on smiling.' (laughter)

In other words keep cheerful, ignore the fact that your village water may be polluted and if you or your family become ill there is no doctor or surgery.

Food, or lack of, still agitated us. On 30 April I wrote:

> *'Came off duty feeling really hungry and what did I find for dinner? A plate of half-cold gristly meat, potatoes and cabbage so old and stale that it had gone brown. Meanwhile we noticed the cooks were preparing themselves a dish of steak and lovely crisp chips.'*

12 May:

> *'Our rations have been cut two or three times this year. Breakfast is mainly baked beans and duck eggs. For the other meal it is mainly tinned meat and tinned vegetables. We do have a nice piece of fish about twice a week, plenty of freshly baked bread and butter, plenty of jam and marmalade, tinned peas and iced water, that's the credit side.*
>
> *On the debit side - a real shortage of vegetables, potatoes (always one tablespoonful or less). The bacon is always tinned small pieces. The meat, all of it, is of poor quality.'*

Apart from the food our main concern was still the climate. On 14 May at 14.00 I recorded a shade temperature of 109.5°F (43°C), the highest so far at Vizag. We were almost gasping for breath, stray dogs lay around panting. Fortunately the humidity was a dry 18 percent. It had been truly said of Madras Province that it had three climates - hot, hotter and hottest.

CHAPTER 28
Typhoid Scare

When I joined 732 FC our roster included one night duty in four. The night duties were not arduous since we slept for a few hours, restless sleep on a first aid stretcher on the ground outside the buildings. There were rats around and once I woke ant-covered.

Initially we did hourly observations, futile really since the 02.00, 03.00 and 04.00 'obs' could not be transmitted until 05.00 so we stopped bothering to do them and made up some figures for the Indian wireless operator to send to Madras.

On 6 May we became a Type 4 Met. Station which meant no charts to plot, but we continued the hourly 'obs'. These took only ten minutes, leaving fifty minutes each hour to read, drink lime juice and chat to the Indian wireless operators. We talked about our respective countries, religion, literature - anything and everything, but above all, India's future. Indian Independence was coming, but when?

When not transmitting morse code the operators used their sets to listen to Indian music. Sometime I took the headphones and thereby acquired a taste for sitars, tablas and the sound of other Indian musical instruments. This was an unusual taste for an Englishman, but today, with a wider interest in world and not just European music, would be unremarkable.

We now had no officers so it was impossible to issue forecasts, which had to be obtained by telephone from St Thomas Mount. For easier contact a telephone was installed in our basha. Most met. assistants were now officerless.

As for flying we normally saw only Dakotas of Transport Command, though on 26 May I recorded:

'Four Spitfires landed - a great event'.

This caused much excitement. Four 'planes at once on our aerodrome!
On 16 May I angrily wrote:

'Why are they keeping us here? We are not occupying Japan, but India. I suppose they are still scared of a further uprising and that Europeans will be attacked. They came out to India of their own accord so let them fend for themselves and not depend on us to back them up. We have no earthly right to be in India, it's the Indian's own country and we have no more grounds for being here than the Nazis had in overrunning France'.

Rather intemperate views and containing over-simplifications, but at the time I was becoming more and more sympathetic to the idea of Indian swaraj (self-rule). I tended to ignore British achievements in India, a Civil Service virtually free of corruption, a comprehensive railway system, the foundations of a democratic form of government that has survived. We did exploit economically, but we also left a valuable legacy.

Next day we had a smallpox vaccination and inoculations against typhus, cholera and typhoid. As I wrote at the time:

'They were done in a hurry because one of the boys is dangerously ill through contracting typhoid. It is believed he caught it through eating ice-cream sold by the contractor. I've eaten pints of the stuff, so I can thank my lucky stars that it was him and not me. The ice-cream is now banned. On camp we expect protection from disease. Considering the way our bread is thrown on the back of the ration lorry it is marvellous that we are as well as we are.'

The 'flap', to use the RAF expression for a panic, began when the airman's typhoid was diagnosed. The first we knew of it was on arrival at the Airmen's Mess, to find a blackboard notice telling us to report to Station Sick Quarters for booster 'jabs'.

Within a few days the first typhoid victim was recovering, but an LAC Budd contracted paratyphoid and died within a week. At his funeral on 4 June the cortege consisted of twelve airmen. I was told at the time for an air commodore it would have been 700. The young man was not a close friend, but I had been chatting to him a day or so before he became ill and I kept seeing his face. We were all badly shaken by his death.

Of course the usual messages would have been sent to his next-of-kin, but what a pointless death. Certainly one thought was now uppermost, survival, until such time as I could leave India.

The lad's death turned my mind to the negative side of India - the disease, the widespread corruption, the tolerance of feudalism, the callous inhumanity of the caste system with high caste Indians being defiled by the mere shadow of those of a lower caste.

What the climate of India could do was clearly illustrated by the case of Ron Trott who I was with at St Thomas Mount. In southern India he endured hell, prickly heat and boils making his life a misery. Soon after I left him, still at St Thomas Mount, he developed malaria. Later he had mid-tour leave. Back in the UK he reported sick, was registered category C3 and declared unfit to return to India. To add to his woes he now had impetigo and ear problems. A consultant said not only should he not have been sent out East, but he should never have been passed as fit for RAF service.

Ron's overseas medical was probably as rudimentary as mine had been at Coltishall at the hands of the Polish MO, when I had not been given an examination of any value. Luckily it did not matter. I survived India with no ill-effects save a tendency on my return home to have bouts of sickness and diarrhoea. This gradually passed.

At Vizag I was to learn a few more things about the RAF Mutiny in which RAF Vizagapatam's airmen had taken part. Evidently they had stayed away from work only for a few hours.

It had been our understanding that as all RAF airmen were working normally the Government and Air Ministry intended to forgive and forget, but possibly we had been misinformed. Certainly investigators were coming to India from the UK intent on finding the ringleaders, or scapegoats, if one wished to be cynical.

Two months after the strike ended one of our 732 FC airmen was closely questioned by RAF police. This was John who, as a known socialist, was a natural choice. As I wrote at the time:

> 'One of our lads was recently questioned from 09.15 - 14.20
> during which time he was asked every conceivable question
> about the strike - and missed his dinner!'

Missing his dinner to me was most important.

One airman, Norris Cymbalist, was imprisoned for his part in the RAF Seletar (Singapore) strike. His sentence was ten years and a handful of others received lesser sentences. These men had been leaders and victimised as such. The sentences were not served in full. As far as Norris Cymbalist was concerned he was released late 1947 thanks to civil liberties activists and trade unionists in Britain.

<u>I wrote at the time of John's interrogation:</u>

> *'The real trouble was not only over release, but also because of bad food, long separation from relatives, bad billets and general lack of comfort.'*

By the end of 1947 few RAF airmen were left in India. Many of the strikers are no longer around and the episode, the legitimate grievance of angry young men, frustrated by the fact that no one was listening, has long since passed into history, little known history.

At the end of May 1,500 'Zombies' or 'Moon Men' arrived at Bombay. Moon Men because of their paleness, but why Zombies? They were 18-year-olds usually with three months or so of RAF service, straight out from the UK, and with demob groups 70 to 74. These lads arrived white-faced and white-kneed as we had done. Ridiculous as it may sound those of us who had been in the RAF for a couple of years or so felt old in comparison to the newcomers. Soon, apart from a few regulars who had signed away several years, there would be few airmen in the whole of the RAF with more than three years service.

By this time I had virtually forgotten what it was like not to be an airman. The monotony of life at Vizag sometimes made me downcast, also we were so isolated and how I missed Madras. For entertainment we relied heavily on the nightly film shows, priced at 6p except at the end of the week when we had more recent films booked directly from a film company (7½p).

If all else failed I could always curl up on my charpoy and read. My April-May reading list was 'Corduroy' by Adrian Bell (Martin's father), Koestler's 'The Yogi and the Commissar,' 'Northanger Abbey' by Jane Austen (I had now read her six main novels. I wished there were sixty!), 'Children of the Earth' by Ethel Mannin, 'The Professor' by Rex Warner and 'Mr Norris Changes Trains' by Christopher Isherwood. Some were bought, others came from the library.

Another source of entertainment was the music circle. We sat outside when possible, under the palm trees and the stars. We listened to Tchaikovsky, Beethoven and other classical composers; played on a wind-up gramophone. I had never appreciated music so much. It carried me out of myself and the sheer beauty of Tchaikovsky's Vth Symphony almost reduced me to tears and still does. This symphony will always link me to Vizag, my friends and our youth, long since gone. Meanwhile the tapes (corporal's stripes) for which I had more than once been recommended, failed to materialise. The extra pay and enhanced gratuity would have been welcome, but meteorology as a trade in India already had the permissible number of corporals. I remained a humble LAC which perhaps gave me a worm's eye view of those above.

CHAPTER 29
Burmese Ramulu

The bearer for our hut was a 14-year-old Burmese lad named Ramulu. He had amazing ability as a tree climber. Our bashas were in a coconut grove and in spite of the lower three-quarters of the trees being branchless Ramulu used to effortlessly climb these palms to obtain for us unripened coconuts used solely for the liquid inside.

Ramulu was good-natured, noisy and roared with laughter at our attempts to speak Hindi. He loved looking at British magazines and liked using his newly-acquired expression:

'What happened?'

If he saw a photo, shall we say of a train crash, out would come 'What happened?' However serious our reply Ramulu treated it all as a wonderful joke.

We usually managed to scrounge a bit of food for Ramulu at the end of our meal in the Airmen's Mess, but had to keep the food well concealed from the sharp eyes of the kite hawks. Only once was I caught off guard, writing on 11 May:

> *'Leaving the cookhouse with bread in my hand for the bearer, I was 'attacked' by a kite hawk. No damage except for a longish scratch on the right hand. It didn't get the bread rolls.'*

A fortnight earlier we had an unwanted visitor in the basha during the night 28/29 April. A thief entered the billet, but must have been scared off by one of the lads. In leaving, the thief must have touched my bed. I was having a nightmare, shot off my charpoy and dived under someone else's mosquito net during my sleep walk. The occupant had quite a shock.

On 25 May someone lost £7 in numbered rupee notes during daylight hours, the 105 rupees representing three week's pay. Theoretically, with

Ramulu guarding our property, this should not have been possible.

My second sleep walk on 26 July ended with me on the floor with one arm twisted under my body. The 'doc' at Station Sick Quarters said it was a sprained elbow. I had it dressed, but for some time found working, washing and dressing none too easy.

But to return to Ramulu, who had his mother and brother living near the aerodrome. All his other relatives had been killed by the Japanese air raids on Rangoon. The war over, the intention was to return to Burma, but Ramulu refused to go so his brother, who would have been older, threatened to beat him. Ramulu left home and made a safe haven for himself somewhere inside the airfield perimeter.

A few weeks later this ostensibly uneducated lad who spoke Burmese, Hindi, Telegu, Tamil and some English, was still at loggerheads with his family.

Ramulu, sad to say, became a bit of a dead loss to us. He was smoking far too much, becoming streetwise and saucy. This eventually turned to cheekiness and laziness and he did less and less work. His duties were to clean shoes, fetch water and make beds, about two or three hours work a day. For this the three of us in the billet each paid one rupee a week. His total wage of 22½p seems derisory and certainly was not generous, but to put it in context a professor at an Indian university would have earned only a few times more.

On 14 November I was robbed of a few pounds, yet curiously enough the thief left me with two Rs10 notes. By day I always had my money with me, whilst at night slept with it under my pillow, so how the thief stole it was a mystery. One possibility was the theft occurred whilst I was having a shower. Harsh as it seemed we decided to change bearers and have someone less cocky and a bit more reliable. Ramulu soon found another employer and we had a new bearer, so all was well. In retrospect it seems strange that even we lower orders of British life in India had a part-share in a servant.

From Ramulu to the USSR seems quite a jump, but around this time my old love of the USSR had totally evaporated and all within twelve months of VE Day. The Soviet Union seemed determined to set up communist satellite states in eastern Europe.

In Germany, a devastated country, the ordinary workers and their families were existing on a minimal amount of food and were paying a high price for Nazism. The 'Manchester Guardian' was alleging that leading German socialists were being sent to Buchenwald the ex-Nazi concentration camp. I now accepted that to the communist Soviet leadership a democratic socialist was as much as enemy as any of the hated capitalists.

I had been duped into believing the USSR to be some kind of socialist paradise, but now realised there was no freedom of the press with 'Izvestia' and 'Pravda', as well as lesser journals, rigidly adhering to the party line. There was no freedom of speech. To allow criticism of the regime would be to encourage alternatives to the one-party state. Even equal educational opportunities for all children did not exist in the way we had been led to believe. The percentage of working-class children in Russian universities was allegedly declining. Soviet officials' children received preferential treatment.

At last the truth had entered my consciousness - 'Uncle Joe' Stalin was a tyrant.

On 9 June I wrote:

> *'I feel perturbed by the turn of events in Europe. The long-awaited peace has brought a return to the old 1939 days of power politics. We are as far off real peace as ever. An armaments race with Russia? Leading of course to one thing - war!'*

22 August 1946:

> *'It (the Cold War) just cannot go on like this for longer than a few years and then will come World War Three. The tragedy is that ordinary Russians and Britons do not hate each other.'*

It did not happen, but we came perilously near it on several occasions.

Any lingering doubts about the Soviet Union were removed when I read 'Darkness at Noon' by Arthur Koestler, an ex-communist. The novel concerned just one victim of the notorious show trials held between 1936 and 1938. My disenchantment was complete, to be replaced by a deep interest in all things Russian and in particular their folk music.

CHAPTER 30
Goodbye Lovely Nilgiris

On 11 June three of us set off for another welcome spell in the Nilgiris, up at 04.00, leaving Vizag at 06.00. The train was a slow one, stopping at every station, a typical Indian train with hard, wooden seats. At the beginning we had a mere handful of passengers, but by the time we reached Madras, the coach (allegedly a military one) was crowded with Madras police and civilians. My two companions decided to move to a second-class coach, already crowded, so I decided to stay with the Indians. It was an experience. Being the only European the Indians eyed me with real interest, obviously talking about me since amidst the local language, Tamil, I caught the odd word 'aeroplane', 'Nilgiris' etc.

One of my companions, an Indian railway-fireman, spoke English and told me he was a Christian. He was especially interested to know that my father was a locomotive driver. He reeled off a list of British drivers he had known. I knew the prominent part Anglo-Indians played in India's railways, but had not realised British crews had been employed. This railwayman's wage was Rs70 (£5.25) per month of which Rs40 went on food, leaving Rs30 to spend on himself, his wife and four children for clothing and necessities. The railwaymen in southern India had recently been on strike and were planning to do so again on 27 June. I wondered if I would be 'caught' up in the Nilgiris unable to report back to Vizag. This would have suited me fine.

In the compartment was an ex-Indian airman, a highly-educated young man with the name Kulshthrestha. He said the name meant 'best in the family'. The equivalent would hardly have been conducive to harmony in a British family. I received an invitation to visit him in Agra, but never did.

We arrived at Madras next day, 29 hours after leaving Vizag, at an average speed of 17 mph. With three hours to spare I caught a tram from Central Station to one of my old haunts, the Chinese restaurant, for a meal of fish and chips followed by banana fritters and iced drinks. Madras was so pleasant compared to Vizagapatam. Returning to Central Station the second stage of the journey began.

Having been given four days ration money at Rs4 (30p) per day I lashed out on reaching Jalarpet Junction buying at the station restaurant a dinner consisting of omelette, chicken and vegetables, followed by a sweet. This cost 20p. Incredibly, at the time, I felt I was really living it up. Today, such is inflation, the amount seems laughable.

The third leg of the journey was on the mountain railway to Wellington. We arrived at Guava Hill, but soon realised it was not as pleasant as Hastings Holiday Home had been. The food, considering that most things could be grown in the varying altitudes of the Nilgiris, was rather poor. The showers, to our surprise, produced only cold water, but it was good to be back in a cool climate, to wear our blue UK uniforms and to sleep under blankets.

The billet being cold we needed to buy wood for the open fire. For this we paid 9p for around 50kg. The poor coolie who carried it up the hill received the standard rate, 4p. Why did we not give him more? To over-pay was regarded as rocking the boat and 'bad form'. We should have ignored it.

It was homely sitting by the fire reading. The billet was a pleasant little building, brick built, with a tiled roof. The walls were distempered cream and yellow (emulsion paint not yet invented). We even had green curtains. I would have settled for this style of living for the rest of my tour.

Not one of the first six days was fine, continual drizzle ruling out any pleasant walks. At the cinema I had my third viewing of 'Pride and Prejudice'. The rest of the time I read novels, having recently 'discovered' George Elliot. It was a pleasing way of passing the time. I had not much in common with many of my associates, the conversation at mealtimes being about as vulgar and low as it could get. In contrast, in Wellington, I spent an interesting couple of hours in the company of an Indian from Madras University talking about novels, films, politics, India and the UK. With the exception of a minority of my fellow-countrymen I had far more in common with English-speaking Indians. The older, mature, sensible BORs had, in the main, gone home and I tired of teenage talk.

I particularly recall one day, 21 June, when I walked the four miles to Coonoor, passing through Sim's Park an area of natural and ornamental gardens, plus woodland. The park had beds of flowers and lily ponds and was so English. A crowd of convent children happily played; no wonder the

British felt so at home in the Nilgiris. I loved it as it was then.

In Coonoor I bought a copy of 'Twelfth Night' and 'The Tempest', the first Shakespeare read since leaving school. There was also a New Testament for me to read. My religious convictions were on the same roller-coaster as my general state of morale. I wavered between belief and unbelief and could not make up my mind about the Christian religion. One Sunday I attended a service at Wellington's parish church. The vicar was so delighted to have had his best ever congregation of seventy, of which around fifty were soldiers.

Two more visits were made to Coonoor, as well as one damp drizzle visit to 'Ooty'. Several times Wellington YMCA was used, a pleasant place and one evening many of us attended a concert given by an RAF group.

The mountain air gave a hearty appetite, but the camp food just had to be supplemented by canteen food which made a hole in the pay.

On 30 June an announcement somehow reached our ears to the effect that anyone who had joined the RAF before 1 January 1944 would be demobbed by 31 December 1947, that is four year's service as a maximum. My hopes of demob before 1948 did not look too promising and this was only mid-1946. To use the RAF expression 'hard cheese' (i.e. tough luck).

On 4 July Guava Hill was left behind and it was down the mountain line. It was always reckoned that the temperature dropped 1°F for each 300 ft (91m). The reverse also applied, so the further we descended the hotter we became.

At Mettupalaiyam we had a five hour wait for the Madras train, the last coach of which was reserved for RAF use. The coach was the worst on the train, being ancient, dirty, smelly and devoid of any glass in the windows. Some RAF comedian had a piece of chalk and expressed the prevailing mood by writing 'cattle' on either side of the coach. This caused some fun for all the English speaking Indians at each station.

In through the windows blew dust and smoke and at night from the crevices out came the red cockroaches, some over five cm long. They were repulsive looking creatures. I cursed Southern India Railway Company and its rolling stock.

The overnight journey ended at Central Station, Madras in time for breakfast at Spencer's. Suitably refreshed it was back to the station for stage three of the journey, this time in an acceptable second-class compartment. Reaching Vizag I was both filthy and tired due to a second night of broken sleep.

128

CHAPTER 31

Vizag Life - Peaceful Isolation and Comradeship

Back at Vizag once more, I found that 'Mac' (Iain) and 'Jock' had improved the basha by the addition of blue net curtains and various wall hangings. For me there was a record haul of mail that included 24 air mail letters, four 'Manchester Guardian' Weeklies and a bundle of 'Daily Heralds', a good popular paper in comparison with some of today's tabloids.

There were changes in Vizag's meteorological contribution. Night duties had been stopped, there was less work to do than ever. Four of our six airmen were to leave soon and the telephone in the billet was to be our main link with other aerodromes. Sometimes in the night Madras would 'phone some totally useless information which we never copied down. When asked to read it back we usually said:

'Thank you Madras.' and put the receiver down.

We did this particularly towards the end of our time when few 'planes landed.

Vizag was as hot as ever, the food much the same. The cooking was now done by only RAF cooks. Indians too faced food problems. An American unofficial food mission had come to India, but a few days earlier their aircraft crashed 18 miles from Vizag, but nobody was hurt.

On 10 July we heard that my best friend, 'Mac' was to be posted to Yelahanka, having completed his twelve months at Vizag. It was pleasing that he was going to a cooler aerodrome, but I would miss his congenial company.

The RAF had now introduced a scheme whereby airmen could sign on for an extra three years, on completion of which a bounty of £100 would be given. Sixty thousand were needed, but so far only two thousand had signed on. The dearth of volunteers could mean some of us staying in a little longer. I had no intention of volunteering for an extra stint.

Apart from the climate and the grotty food, life at Vizag was tolerable. Providing we carried out our far from onerous duties we did as we liked. We lived in our own little world and I was able to read for many hours each week. There was enough money for my modest needs, mainly books and food. Above all there was the comradeship of friends, a kind of brotherhood never known before or since. Vizag was, for the present, a relaxed station - but I was soon to change my tune.

On 15 July a murder took place in a basha 200 yards from mine. A coolie cut the throat of a ten-year-old-boy and stole a few silver coins. One life ended for so little money. The murderer was caught, but how desperate he must have been to kill a child in this way for such a pittance. In what low esteem life was held in India.

On such a sad day there was a welcome item of good news. The Indian tour for single men was being reduced from three years to two years six months. My tour could go on no longer than 2 November 1947, assuming I was not demobbed before that date, or posted home.

Two days later we had a second death, an Indian airman being accidentally electrocuted. There was dangerous wiring all over the aerodrome. We had only had electric lighting in our basha for a comparatively short time, but all wiring had to be removed as a precaution. The alternative would have been some rewiring, but I believe the RAF knew Vizag's days were numbered and electrical work would have been wasted money. The RAF had already left St Thomas Mount. But for us the stripping of the wiring meant a return to oil lamps, wonderful for attracting insects.

Our basha was, as I have mentioned, in a coconut grove, but we also had a tree that produced a strange fruit, something like a blackcurrant. One morning, near naked as usual, I rose from my charpoy to find thirteen pairs of mainly female eyes watching my every move. The fruit gatherers, like all Indians, had an innate sense of curiosity and watched fascinated as I squeezed toothpaste onto my brush. I asked in broken (very broken!) Telegu what were they looking at and received some sheepish smiles.

This sense of curiosity had a funny side. One of my friends was travelling on a tram in Madras. He had a parcel on his lap and he swore that an Indian had undone the parcel to see the contents, neatly retied the string and handed the brown paper parcel back to its owner profusely thanking him.

The monsoon in one spell gave four successive days of rain.
On 23 July I wrote:

130

'Here I am in my old basha with the rain pouring down and trying my best to write by the light of an oil lamp. Bullfrogs are croaking and numerous insects are appearing with the monsoon rains. It has rained almost continuously for four days now and everything one touches is damp and clammy. There is nowhere to dry anything without a fire and our usual source of heat, the sun, has been hidden by clouds for days. There is one consoling factor - the temperature. For once the temperature has been reasonable and on occasions has been below 80°F (27°C). The usual maximum temperature here is 85°F-95°F (29-35°C).'

When it was hot and damp, as happened so frequently, writing letters was difficult. To prevent smudging we always put blotting paper under the non-writing arm.

Two large fruitbats had been electrocuted on the overhead wire that passed over our billet. Their screams were horrible. They now hung on the wires with flies buzzing around them. We avoided walking under them in case one fell.

There were also pretty little chipmunks playing outside the billet. They were rather like squirrels and by laying a trail of peanuts it was possible to entice them inside. Some of them became quite tame.

Water buffalo wandered amongst the palms, on one occasion one came into the basha leaving as a visiting card large dollops of dung. The next visitation was by night. Although stark naked, I jumped out of bed, put on my chappalies (sandals) and chased it out of the billet and through the coconut grove into the distance, to the laughter of my billet mates.

Once I spotted a species of owl on the basha roof, but usually we saw only the usual crows and pariah kites plus some colourful birds that had pathetic 'songs'. Vultures looking like wizened old men occasionally wheeled overhead.

Very occasionally we had snakes in the billet, usually quite harmless creatures, but there was little else in the way of wild life apart from the numerous insects that pestered us by day and night. If global warming means a hotter Britain we may have some unwanted insect visitors.

On 2 August the new Transport Command schedule started. We were now to receive a northbound and southbound Dakota on alternate days. These Dakotas were our main link with the outside world bringing our eagerly awaited letters. These now came via a different route i.e. Karachi - New Delhi - Calcutta - Vizagapatam. Previously the route had been Bombay - Bangalore - Madras - Vizag.

Only two of us were now doing the work of 732 FC, working alternate mornings and afternoons. It seemed inconceivable that the RAF found justification for keeping two hundred men on an aerodrome that saw one aircraft a day. Three days in August a Dakota arrived with just one passenger on board. We seemed to be operating a glorified taxi service to ensure that high-ranking RAF and Army Officers could avoid train travel.

Late August we were told that rifle training would start which, considering the communal violence, was a wise precaution. But I would have thought very hard at this time before firing at an Indian and would have done so only in extremis. The sten gun I had brought with me to India had been handed in at St Thomas Mount.

Vizagapatam had been put out of bounds because of a sweepers' strike and for six weeks I had not moved more than two miles from the basha. For a break there was an occasional film and one evening we joined the IORs to see an Indian film. The few BORs in the audience were closely observed; the Indians studied our reactions. I also attended an Indian variety show and found the music enjoyable.

More and more I associated with Indian airmen, which reminds me of a story at the time. An RAF Officer in the UK was evidently warning a group of WAAFs about airmen coming back from India. He described the airmen as being ninety per cent mad and ten per cent pro-Indian. I was certainly in the latter category, perhaps also the former.

The ways of the RAF took some fathoming. On 26 August we handed in our respirators and steel helmets. The gas masks we had pointlessly carried around in our kit bags for a whole post-war year. But with the increasing unrest it would have seemed logical to have retained our 'tin hats'. The arms training did not take place which caused no surprise. RAF proposals often did not come to fruition and even if begun often petered out.

Mid-July I had applied for a Modern Citizenship course. The course to be held at Darjeeling consisted of three weeks of lectures and discussions. Darjeeling was a thousand miles from Vizag and being in the hills had a lovely cool climate and would have made a pleasant break. Few applied, but only one was selected from Vizag, and that was not me.

My application had not been helped by the fact that for a time I was nominally in charge of the unit - all three of us. The corporal was away and I took over, though technically only an NCO could be in charge. The RAF sent plenty of junk mail (forms etc.). If it looked important I dealt with it, though most was confined to the waste bin. That there was no comeback was a measure of its importance.

The strike of the Sweepers Union continued and the city remained off-limit. A short letter signed 'Inhabitant' was published in a local paper which ran as follows:

'I would like to ask the Sweepers' Union here why the inhabitants of this city are boycotted when the strike is against the municipality.

The city has no sanitary latrines. The sweepers will not work in houses, nor will they allow houses to be cleaned.

They have succeeded in making the city into a slum and they ask us to sympathise.'

Cleaning was a low caste occupation, not to be engaged in by higher castes. Did the upper caste houses stay unclean?

The strike over I visited Vizag again on 20 September:

'It's the first time I've been down there for weeks and the place hasn't improved at all. Where Vizag is concerned absence does not make the heart grow fonder.

There, amidst all the stink and filth, children were rushing around half naked, the dogs were scrounging amongst the rubbish, the beggars, the rickshaw-pullers - the whole teeming mass of Vizag, just one drop in India's colossal population of 400 million.

An hour or so in the town, amidst the odour and under the sweltering sun, was enough for me with my shirt hanging on my back like a damp cloth. RAF Vizag is a haven of peace in comparison to the rest of India.'

So much for Vizagapatam, my least favourite Indian place.

On the aerodrome the vexed question of food, or the lack of, still rankled with us as these comments show.

26 July:

'Main meal today - meat, three pieces the size normally put in a stew, a tablespoon of peas. No potatoes. Second course - a small piece of pudding.'

<u>27 July:</u>

> *'We have seen no fresh vegetables for weeks and have been living on dehydrated potatoes, baked beans and tinned meat.'*

<u>30 July:</u>

> *'The food is grim and none too plentiful. The everlasting monotony of dehydrated food is bad enough, but when it is in short supply the position is even worse.'*

<u>16 August:</u>

> *'An airman's breakfast (06.30 feeling hungry!)*
> *Porridge - thick, unsweetened and full of insects.*
> *Bacon - four small pieces, about enough to fill a teaspoon.*
> *Rissole - made of fried bully beef.*
> *Bread - sticky, smelly and full of insects (dead ones!). Too unpleasant to eat more than one slice.'*

And in this way the meals continued, poor in quality and quantity, the worst I had ever had in the RAF.

<u>2 October:</u>

> *'Breakfast: Unsweetened porridge. One small slice of bacon and two dessert spoons of soggy, dehydrated potatoes.*
> *Midday meal: Half a slice of cheese, a quarter ounce or less, (7 grams), half a slice of spam, a dessert spoonful of salmon, four slices of apricot (one spoonful).*
> *On this we are expected to live. Most are too scared to complain. Told the Orderly Officer the other day that I hadn't enough food and he got me another plateful. The reason we don't starve is because out of our own pockets we buy toast and cakes at the canteen and a hot supper at night. Why should we spend over half our pay on food which the RAF is supposed to supply.'*
> *By the time RAF food has passed through the hands of crooked persons and bad cooks there is little left to eat.'*

<u>5 October:</u>

> *'Showdown on the camp. The CO called some of the boys together and heard their grievances about food. The CO agreed that the food was bad. The boys expressed their opinion that some of our food is being stolen and some is wasted by the cooks. Certainly it goes somewhere and I'm certain we don't*

have our full ration. Our sugar comes to a negligible quantity during the week. Most of the tea is unsweetened and we never have food that could possibly contain sugar. Where does it go? Since the complaint to the CO the tea has suddenly become comparatively sweet.'

Significant! To be fair, from this time onwards food did improve somewhat, but in retrospect had we presented a united front more could have been done, but unity was not evident. I witnessed a good example of this when an officer came round at breakfast asking if we had any complaints. I told him the porridge tasted horrible. He looked shocked, did the rounds, had no further complaints and came back to tell me so. No one else had actually complained, yet on my table alone were three plates of uneaten porridge, which the officer should have spotted.

One day rice was on the menu. Being the staple diet of Indians in Madras Province the RAF had been told never to serve it to BORs. Since protesting to my superiors was a waste of time my local MP was informed. No more rice.

The food at one stage was so dire that we were issued with tablets to supplement the inadequate diet, probably vitamins.

CHAPTER 32
The Great Calcutta Killings

On 20 August 1946 I wrote that two hundred people had been murdered in Calcutta where Muslims and Hindus were fighting. This period one historian calls 'The Great Calcutta Killings.'

On 25 August I recorded:

> *'Troubles recently in Calcutta between Hindus and Muslims have led to the deaths of over two thousand people with several thousand wounded. In the RAF there are Hindu and Muslim airmen living together peacefully. It is only the fanatics who kill one another.*
>
> *Muslims live principally in Northern India and their leader, Mr Jinnah, thinks Muslims should have their own state. The arguments against the creation of the separate Muslim state (Pakistan) are many. In the first place there would be millions of Hindus living in Pakistan and likewise Muslims in India. The Muslims seem determined to have a separate state and Mr Jinnah's Muslim League are pressing for it.*
>
> *The Hindu Congress under Mr Nehru is against any partition of India and I cannot help agreeing with them. The Hindus realise the stupidity of splitting India, since the country's whole economic life would be affected by so drastic a change. Anyway, whatever their differences it is no solution to take up arms while Indians remain so poverty-stricken and in need of peace.*
>
> *The Indians near here are living in desperate poverty. Many live entirely off their little pieces of land and are in the grips of tyrannical landlords. The landlords lend these people money at appalling rates of interest and when the peasant*

cannot repay he loses his home and property. The Indian is forced to move to a city where he begs for his living.'

In the above account I did not mention the large number of Muslims in east India, the power of money-lenders over Indian peasants borrowing for weddings and so forth. The Indian having lost his land then moved to a town to work, failing that he begged in order to survive. I am sure nothing has changed in cities such as Calcutta.

29 August:

'The Calcutta riots have quietened down. Up to Monday 3,468 bodies were removed from streets, hospitals, sewers, canals and rivers. Probably four thousand at least were injured, and the figures do not include bodies taken from the streets by relatives. Indians generally are as shocked by the carnage as much as we are.'

The Calcutta riots began on the night 15/16 August. Jinnah's Muslim League declared 16 August a Day of Action and a hartal, a hartal being a general strike. The night before Muslim mobs armed with iron bars and any tool that could be used as a weapon mercilessly killed any Hindus in sight. Later Hindus retaliated and acted with the same brutality.

The Calcutta killings, with an estimated six thousand deaths, only ended when British troops moved in and guess who had the revolting task of removing ten-day-old corpses? Why the good old Tommies. People there at the time have told me of swollen corpses in the waters of the river Hooghly. Vultures performed their scavenger role sitting on the floating bodies.

In October I wrote of looting and killing at Noakhali in Bengal.

23 October:

'In the province of Bengal Muslims outnumber Hindus. The Muslims have been attacking and killing Hindus. Homes have been robbed, women abducted and forced to become Mohammedans. The Muslims make me impatient and although I try to view things fairly and impartially I am beginning to sympathise with the Hindus. The Hindus are less warlike than the Muslims and less fanatical.'

East Bengal eventually became part of Pakistan, then in 1971 broke away to become Bangladesh.

My viewpoint may have been coloured by a greater association with RIAF Hindus than Muslims. The ramifications of Indian politics I only

137

partly understood.   Although Hindus appeared to tolerate other religions it was unfair to see Muslims as warlike and Hindus as non-violent.   When it came to Partition in 1947 both Hindus and Sikhs did some barbaric things to Muslims and they in turn acted with equal ferocity and callousness. Gandhi was appalled by his Hindu co-religionists. What an extraordinary man he was - a spiritual leader to millions of Indians, a man who by fasting or merely threatening a fast exerted an enormous influence.   Others had a different perception of him, but personally his assassination on 30 January 1948 left me shocked and saddened.

CHAPTER 33

Memories of Dakotas, and No Aeroplanes at all

The few aircraft that landed at Vizag were almost all Dakotas carrying one or two passengers and on 31 August I wrote of a Dakota that had arrived two days previously:

> *'After refuelling and giving the passengers time for breakfast it was ready to take-off. Just as the engines warmed up I received an emergency message from Calcutta to say the weather was bad up there. I had to pass on the 'gen' to Flying Control who stopped the 'plane from taking off. It should be leaving tomorrow at 05.30.*
>
> *The aircrew had been rather annoyed to stay at Vizag for two days and grumbled quite a bit believing of course that the weather wouldn't have stopped <u>them</u>. That's the same with all aircrew, they are prepared to fly however bad the weather, rather than wait for it to improve.'*

Perhaps they did not like Vizag's comforts, but there was often a suggestion of a curious love-hate relationship between meteorologists and those who flew. Inaccurate forecasts were remembered.

Early in September 1946 140 extra airmen arrived, virtually doubling our BOR population. These men had just returned from mid-tour leave in the UK. All were barracked together in a spare cookhouse, beds being pushed together within a few inches of each other, but at least they had electric lighting. Our Airmen's Mess became quite crowded and we even queued for meals.

From the men we heard at first hand about life in the UK. Back home things were no better than during the war, with the same rationing, the same queues and even common items in short supply.

The day before they left, the transit lads had a football match against RAF Vizag which the latter won 5-1. My friend 'Mac' played a blinder in midfield and I was amazed that he could stand the pace in such a climate.

Our visitors sailed next day from Vizagapatam's harbour to Malaya and we returned to our quiet, lonely existence.   Meantime, as a staging post, our usual six Dakota landings had now been cut to four per week, the Monday and Friday flights from Calcutta bringing the coveted mail.   The sound of the approaching Dakota was synonymous with letters, an evocative sound.   To think some are still flying over sixty years after it came into service as a US airliner.

On Sunday, 15 September we had a commemorative Battle of Britain parade, the sixth anniversary.   The parade was not to our liking.   We were unused to parades and felt foolish marching around the camp.   It was not as if there were any civilians to look on.   Anyway the CO said a few words about the sacrifices of the young pilots of Fighter Command in 1940 and had a dig at those who, six years later, just grumbled.   What us?   We ended with a prayer for the RAF.

The same day one of our Dakota visitors took off for Calcutta at 11.00, but six hours later returned to Vizag having run into trouble.   The pilot had almost reached Calcutta, but ran into a heavy storm and sensibly turned back.

RAF Vizagapatam on a busy day - three Dakotas at once!
To left a civil airliner. The other two are RAF transports.

He had faced a massive bank of cumulonimbus clouds that he could neither fly over, nor round. The passengers had a rough trip and most instruments were out of order. We half expected a crash and the ambulance was ready, but to our great relief a successful landing was made.

Next day the Dakota took off, but again failed to reach Calcutta because of bad weather. This time the pilot landed at an aerodrome a hundred miles short of his destination. The monsoon period was bad weather for flying, but sometimes pilots ignored meteorological advice. Even in those far off days the Met. Office forecasts were usually correct. There were exceptions of course, well remembered, but meteorology is not an exact science.

One particular Dakota incident stands out in my memory. Our facilities for night landings were rudimentary to say the least, oil lamps being placed at the side of the runway. Since so few 'planes came, and those only in daylight, the oil lamps had been 'borrowed' by the officers to decorate an outside drinking spot.

One evening a Dakota flew from Madras intent on landing at Vizag - in darkness. Panic ensued. A signal was sent asking the crew to return to Madras, but communication by radio was lost and it was now clear that the Dakota was on the way and <u>had</u> to land at Vizag. An almighty 'flap' then ensued. Airmen in a lorry were hurriedly despatched to the Officers' Mess to dismantle the fairy grotto and illuminate the runway for the approaching aircraft.

The Dakota would be aided by a flashing airfield identification beacon giving our call-sign. The light was attached to a purpose-built vehicle, but initially no one knew how to operate it. I gave them the benefit of my mechanical experience by looking on. Eventually, someone solved the problem, and the landing was made without mishap, to sighs of thankfulness all round. We had a chuckle about it afterwards though.

With Vizagapatam town now again in bounds some of our number began visiting prostitutes. Two of our eighteen-year-olds had been caught in a Vizag brothel several weeks earlier by station police. They were marched before the CO who took a dim view of it and sentenced them to seven days 'jankers' (drill etc.). Around ten per cent of our BORs had been taking advantage of a risky association with these young ladies. The CO did not want this to go on since, apart from the moral considerations, by contracting VD they were damaging RAF property!

The CO decided to take us in groups to tour the brothel scene, a kind of red light area guided tour, the idea being to put us off. 'Jock' had his turn, but the scheme fell through before my visit came. My curiosity was never satisfied. Why did so many RAF schemes just fizzle out? It happened so often. 'I have a cunning plan.........' Ah, but will it work? If it does, will it be brought to a conclusion?

Mid-September a Gurkha regiment arrived to share our site and their part of the camp now reeked of 'bull'. We could hear morning reveille and other bugle calls. There was much marching. This quite appalled us since we feared all this military display might give our officers ideas, which was the last thing we wanted. Any disturbance of our easy-going way of life was decidedly unwelcome.

These tough little Nepalese of the 8th Regiment of the Gurkha Rifles were ardently pro-British and gave us broad grins of real affection when we met. Their loyalty to Britain was legendary.

At this time we had no MO, if taken ill, and no dentist either. In the past Vizag airmen had been flown to Bangalore for dental treatment, later being sent, again by aeroplane, to Secunderabad in the state of Hyderabad. This was a good method of getting away for a few days. Genuinely needing some fillings I was sent to see the Gurkha MO who said my teeth were fine which was so obviously untrue. So now it was not possible to get dental treatment. By persistence I managed to visit a neighbouring Army unit where an Indian Army dentist did the necessary work using a pedal-operated drill.

Late September we were told the status of Vizag was being reduced to that of a Care and Maintenance unit. This would require just a skeleton staff with all others being posted. Those that remained might not even be sufficient to service the few aircraft that flew in. This handful of landings hardly justified two hundred of us. The RAF was now in a transition period from war to peace, but seemed to us so disorganised. For example it was said that the Madras-Calcutta route now had only one complete aircrew, yet there were dozens of trained crew members doing ground jobs.

At twenty I was now older than ninety per cent of Vizag's airmen so many 'eighteens' having been sent out.

On 23 October I wrote:

> *'During the past fortnight I have not seen one aeroplane. The regular service through Vizag has stopped owing to the Dakota being out of order.*
> *An aerodrome near Calcutta has had two crashes this last*

week, one aircraft crashing at the end of the runway. There are far too many accidents occurring here for air travel to be really safe. I'm keeping to the solid earth.'

It was in fact several weeks before we actually even saw an aeroplane, not even one in the sky. The Dakotas were being used to drop food to East Bengal's homeless victims of the floods. The land in the Ganges delta was virtually at sea level and notoriously prone to flooding, as it still is.

But to return to our friends the Gurkhas. Their CO commissioned the erection of a large shield outside the HQ of the 8th Gurkha Rifles. It was to consist of the previously mentioned shield emblazoned with their emblem, crossed kukris. The kukri was the curved knife which broadened towards the point, a vicious looking weapon.

The Gurkha shield evidently led our own CO to toy with the idea of our own SHQ emblem. It was rumoured that it was to be a propeller, not too appropriate since we no longer saw aeroplanes at Vizag. Did we have our unit emblem? Well, of course not.

Our Transport Command Dakotas were becoming old as our Corporal, Tommy, found out. He wished to travel from Vizagapatam to Yelahanka and, if possible, to avoid an uncomfortable rail journey. By good fortune a Dakota landed, flown by a Free French crew and it's destination was none other than Yelahanka. Would they mind giving him an air lift? They agreed, no problem.

The crew made navigation easy by hugging the coastline of the Bay of Bengal. Periodically, to Tommy's mounting consternation, the crew threw pieces of the Dakota overboard into the sea. This bizarre procedure continued, item following item. The lone passenger by now was convinced that his life was in the hands of crazy men. To his relief they did actually reach Yelahanka, but the pilot would not have his Dakota serviced or refuelled. The reason was simple enough, the Dakota was past the sell-by-date, or should we say fly-by date and was being delivered to an aircraft graveyard to become scrap metal.

What a strange place Vizag airfield was. We had little work to do and normally operated a three-day work cycle - afternoon duty, morning duty, day off. Even mid-afternoon it was deathly quiet, no aeroplanes, no distant sound of motor traffic, just the wind and an occasional train. Only a handful of us were on the airfield, the rest (cooks, drivers, police etc.) being at camp two miles away.

143

Occasionally we heard jackals on the airfield, but usually only when doing a night duty. They hunted in packs, being seldom seen by day, though on one occasion six came within a hundred yards of Flying Control. I managed to move some 20 - 30 yards from them before they scampered off.

It was a strange place that airfield. There was a deep sense of solitude, almost of inner peace. Although I will never do so I would love to see it again, though some of the memories would be painful, of young men, many of whom are no longer around. Why is it that with advancing years comes this yearning to revisit the scenes of one's youthful past, with old men returning to battlefields often for 'one last look'?

Vizag's climate still concerned me. Somehow the damp heat was just about bearable by day, but was detestable at night and I longed for East Anglia's coolness. Here in September it was awfully hot and the customary prickly heat was playing up my back and shoulders. Describing night temperatures I wrote:

> '70° at night is perfect, 75° tolerable, 80° unpleasant and 85° is hell'

i.e. 21°C, 24°C, 27°C and 29°C.

On 17 October we had a weather panic. A cyclone over the Bay of Bengal was heading in Vizag's direction. We told some of the non-met. personnel and rumours spread, becoming worse in the telling until everyone was convinced the buildings were about to be demolished by the wind. Some time earlier at RAF Gannavaram the winds had taken off the roofs of bashas, the occupants being forced out into torrential rain.

The CO 'phoned the office asking for meteorological details and being responsible for everyone's safety, ordered all airmen to move into stone buildings. Being a member of the awkward squad I decided to stay put in my basha where it was at least quiet; foolish really. We did have strong winds and heavy rain, but no serious damage was done. Why was I so awkward?

Next day the wind had somewhat abated, but it was damp and drizzly. Rain at Vizag seemed so depressing. Decaying vegetation and the thatch of our bashas gave a mustier smell than usual.

Our orders at this time said that during the evening we must wear long slacks and shirt sleeves had to be down. In the heat it was a temptation to strip off. One evening I sat shirtless in the canteen when in walked the CO. He could have put me on a charge for disobeying an order, but instead was decent about it. He asked how long I had been in India. When I answered he gave me a look as if to say 'you ought to know better'. With the remark: 'You've been in India six months longer than I have', he slung the shirt at me and walked out.

The CO combined strictness with a sense of humour and had made an effort to improve conditions. He came round the canteen every evening, which was more than his fellow officers ever did.

Although I had been too young to vote I was politically aware enough to regard myself as a socialist. I approved of the nationalisation of coal mines and railways, even so I had my own reservations about our Labour Government. I disliked the slow rate of demobilisation and its inconsistencies. Then on 8 August 1946 we were told of the new 'improved' pay scales. More disillusion.

My pay in present day currency had been 30p per day, plus 5p Japanese Campaign Pay. The new rate was 35p per day, plus 3p allowance for being overseas. Theoretically I gained 3p per day. In point of fact I was worse off. The exchange rate in India had been fixed at Rs15 for £1. Now we were to receive only Rs13.25 to the pound, which left me slightly worse off (one rupee). Back in the UK I would have gained 21p a week.

At this time I was paying income tax at the rate of one old penny a day - in present currency £1.50 per annum, which hardly justified the collection of such a trifling amount.

CHAPTER 34
Vizag 'Winter' 1946 - 1947

Early in November it seemed that our days at Vizagapatam were numbered since 732 FC would be moving to Tambaram just a few miles south-west of St Thomas Mount, so it would be back to Madras once more. We acquired a Commanding Officer, an Indian F/O Ramamurthy. Although I got my tongue round <u>his</u> name, to him I was always Lowday.

November saw the dismissal of 150 civilians employed by RAF Vizag. Many were chowkidars (guards). None of them had received much pay, but the loss of even a small wage was a disaster to these local village men. The guarding, for the time that Vizag remained open, would be done by night patrols of three airmen riding in a car. I did one such patrol.

Physical training was introduced. At one stage we had to assemble on the football field and run to the Guardroom a mile away. From there we ran back to the field where we were given a chit to prove completion of the not very arduous run. Only on production of the piece of paper were we entitled to any breakfast. As expected, these runs before breakfast, only continued for a few days then stopped.

The discipline at Vizag tightened up and with so many eighteens it was easier to enforce. The corporals were instructed to be more aloof and to eat at separate tables. Some of the officers did their best to be severe. Hats had to be worn by day with no socks round the ankles. One young IOR served seven days 'jankers' for sending an unauthorised message on his W/T set. In the absence of gainful employment the wireless-operators were in the habit of sending messages to friends at other aerodromes.

Another Indian was given ten days confinement, reporting to the Guardroom on the hour every evening to do useful work - such as polishing bomb cases! He had arrived at SHQ two minutes late for duty. Witnesses backed his statement that it was only two minutes, but the CO disagreed.

Anyway late was late, but some months earlier it would have been overlooked.

The grapevine reported that at Yelahanka an airman was caught with socks one inch too low in relationship to the kneecaps. Fourteen days confined to barracks was his punishment. It was all becoming rather nit-picking and petty.

November brought cooler weather. Unlike northern India where temperatures would fall to 50°F - 60°F, in southern India the seasonal variation was less marked. Even so it was good to have daytime maximums never above 90°F (32°C). At night it was cool enough to cover oneself with a sheet and, as winter progressed, even a blanket. I so wished the short Indian winters could be as lengthy as that searing, relentless, seemingly endless hot season.

One November evening I watched with the IORs an Indian show consisting mainly of songs and dances with both male and female performers. In my words:

> *'Of the five girls, two in particular were really lovely. Their hair was long and dark, black eyes, light brown skins and more graceful than the average English girl.*

RAF Vizagapatam September 1946, flying-control (Met. office on left).

Lots of Indian girls, particularly from the upper classes, are most beautiful. They are so graceful and I cannot wonder that a few Englishmen stay out here and marry one. Indian people have such lovely teeth and on stage a girl's smile appears as a flash of dazzling white.'

Around Vizag the only females we normally saw were the dark-skinned, overworked and underfed local women toiling in the fields, poor creatures. We seldom saw middle and upper class women. They led sheltered, protected lives and were not allowed the degree of freedom enjoyed by their British counterparts.

There was no fraternisation between these young ladies and British servicemen. The Indian women were shy and aloof, though at times we were closely watched in the remoter villages. As far as I could see the only social contact for RAF BORs was with Anglo-Indians. Derek at St Thomas Mount had been going out with an Anglo-Indian, but it was always said that if we did have an association with an Indian girlfriend one soon got posted elsewhere. I never knew anyone who put it to the test, the barriers and opportunities just did not make it feasible.

Arranged marriages between Indians were commonplace and usual. One

RAF Vizagapatam Jack, Lewis and someone not remembered by name.

148

of my Indian friends received a letter from his parents, who suggested it was time he married. They enclosed two photos of young ladies and offered him a choice. I was surprised these liberated your RAF men would accept this. Equally surprising was that both sets of parents consulted astrologers as an integral part of the engagement plans.

On 15 November we visited the Hindu temple at Simhachelam, the trip being organised by the CO. Seventy of us travelled the few miles in lorries. The temple in a prominent position in the Kailasa Hills gave a clear view of our distant airfield.

Having mounted almost a thousand steps we removed our shoes and did our best to avoid the dung dropped by two cows that wandered quite freely. Part of the temple was off-limits to us and the marriage chamber containing a figure made of gold was railed off.

The principal room had its walls lined with garish animal-like figures. Without being disrespectful I was reminded of the brightly-painted animals on a fairground roundabout. The temple roof was made partly of gold and allegedly had a value of one million rupees (£75,000 in 1946). I remember thinking the poor could make better use of the money, but what of silverware in English Churches?

The temple was the place of worship attended by some of my RAF friends. Our airmen in stockinged feet wandered most respectfully and treated the temple with dignity. My lasting impression was the smell of manure and incense and a riot of colour. Perhaps I was too familiar with our mediaeval Norfolk village churches, always so peaceful and uncluttered, though more colourful in former times.

After descending the steps we found the CO handing out ice-

Guptan, Wireless-Operator RIAF

creams and lime drinks, the first ice-cream since the typhoid scare. The gesture was kind and much appreciated.

One evening I took a long walk with the wireless-operator, Guptan. It was a moonlit evening and in that light the villages looked picturesque. The beauty of India was there, but one was so conscious of the all-pervading atmosphere of grinding poverty. But this was a time of festival and sounds of music came from the villages we passed. From Guptan I had learnt many things about Indian life and customs. He was a high-caste Brahmin, a cultivated little man who was a poet in his own tongue, Malayalam. When on leave in Kerala he was always embarrassed by the subservience of the low-caste Hindus employed on his father's estate. He told these people there was no need to leave the footpath when he approached. He did his best to let these people know that in his eyes they were his equals, but all to no avail.

When my lethargy allowed, I was learning German using a correspondence course supplied by the Pelman Institute. I had loathed French lessons at school, having no liking for the sarcasm of the teacher, a man who could humiliate. I liked the German language and my failure in French gave me an added incentive in my studies. I soon proved to myself that I could learn a foreign language and was not linguistically handicapped.

CHAPTER 35
Christmas 1946 at Vizagapatam

The Christmas spent at Vizag was my third in the RAF. I missed the cool, crisp British air, carol singers, holly - but above all one's own people. It was now eight years since my last peacetime Christmas in 1938, when I was just twelve. To celebrate, the three of us in the billet, ordered two 2lb Christmas cakes purely for own consumption. We must surely have sickened of it.

The Christmas Eve cinema show was memorable and gave a foretaste of things to come. Many of the audience were drunk. Some were noisy, others insensible, some dozed peacefully, some were vomiting, whilst one lay flat on his back hiccuping. The film, which a few of us actually saw, was 'Rake's Progress' which, in the circumstances, was an apt choice.

On Christmas Day, apart from an hour or so at the airfield checking the instruments, I was free. The airfield was lonelier than ever.

The cooks did us proud, even for breakfast, serving us bacon and tomatoes. Immediately afterwards we watched the IORs Airmen's Mess burn down, due it was later found to faulty electrical wiring - what a surprise! Some of my Indian friends had been inside, but made a swift exit. The RAF fire tender arrived, but was unable to raise enough water pressure for the hoses, so the civilian fire service was notified. By the time a fire engine arrived from Vizag town the building was a smouldering mass of charred wood. In such a normally dry climate buildings constructed mainly of wood and thatch soon burnt down.

The old hands at St Thomas Mount told the tale of a toilet block deliberately burnt down one Christmas Day during the war. This was in the days when men were still doing overseas tours of four years and many were totally frustrated by long absence from families. I was told that having set fire to the toilet the men then joined hands and danced round singing a bawdy song they had made up.

The fire over, we moved to the football pitch where the Officers versus Sergeants football match was to be played. It was a mixture of rugby and soccer, the players wearing pyjamas, pullovers and miscellaneous items such as life-jackets. No one knew who was winning, there being no rules. At one point someone decided to fix up a hosepipe and drenched the players. Not satisfied with this, one of the officers was placed on a stretcher and overturned in the thickest mud. This really pleased us since the 'targeted' officer was one who had been dishing out punishments for petty offences.

Entertainment over we turned up at the Airmen's Mess for our Christmas dinner where we were served by the now clean and mud-free officers and sergeants. The diners as usual enjoyed the occasion and some took delight in ordering around the 'waiters', though some airmen went over the top.

The meal according to my menu consisted of tomato soup, turkey, potatoes and peas, being rounded off by Christmas pudding and mincepies. Those RAF meals at Christmas were always good, even though the palm tree setting was odd. I wonder how many others kept their menu?

That Christmas a few of us were given garlands by the canteen staff. We wore these decorations of flowers and coloured baubles round our necks.

RAF Vizagapatam Christmas Day 1946.
Garlands for Jack, Tommy and Lewis - a gift from the canteen owner.

They were a token of affection and respect. The Indians realised only too clearly which BORs treated them with courtesy and fairness and gave garlands accordingly. The garlands were thin on the ground at Vizag that Christmas.

At this point I was almost two-thirds of my way through the tour. There had been miserable days when my body was in India, but my heart was at home. In spite of the heat and periods of inactivity when our very presence seemed a waste of RAF personnel, I had enjoyed a fair measure of contentment and peace of mind.

Towards the end of 1946 we received a foolish order that no airman was to possess more than one blanket, all others to be handed in. Now, in the absence of a mattress, we habitually slept with a blanket under us as well as a sheet. Otherwise we would have had an uncomfortable night, since we were virtually lying on criss-crossed ropes. In the short-lived winter we sometimes needed a blanket on top, so it was a necessity to own two.

My second blanket had been given to me by someone going home on demob. I had no intention of handing it in to stores, so disobeyed the order and hid the blanket by day. This all seems so petty and not worth recording, but is a typical instance of what irritated us about some RAF decisions that had not been thought through.

To be fair to the RAF we were given some wonderful opportunities for self-improvement. My study of German was immensely aided by the arrival at the Education Section of a German Linguaphone course. We had acquired a gramophone of the old HMV wind-up type, so by playing the records I could hear correct pronunciation. There was no EVT at Vizag, but good educational opportunities existed at each RAF aerodrome and the Education officers were always helpful. The facilities always included a good selection of books, though the majority made no use of what was available, which I could never understand.

CHAPTER 36
The Royal Indian Air Force Mutiny at Vizagapatam

On 2 January 1946 a concert was to have been held for the Indian airmen, but it was boycotted because of the allegedly high admission price. This must have put the officers in a somewhat embarrassing situation.

Next day a photograph was to be taken of the entire personnel. As we lined up two British Officers walked behind making crude remarks about the Indians who were 'silly bastards', our 'black brethren' and so on, all meant to amuse the BORs. They were just playing up to our white airmen many of whom were anti-Indian and needed no encouragement. I seethed and audibly muttered my disapproval, then thought it wiser to shut up. The arrogance and ignorance of the two officers, one of whom was the CO, seemed to me no different than the Herrenvolk (master race) attitude the Nazis had shown.

As a punishment for boycotting the concert the CO put the IORs recreation room out of bounds, cancelled all Indian film shows and made the Indians parade.

On 4 January no Indians turned up for meals and they began a hunger strike. My offer to bring a few of them some food was turned down with typically eloquent expressions of gratitude. At the time I failed to understand that these young men were employing Mahatma Gandhi's philosophy of satyagraha, the force of truth, that is non-violent resistance.

That afternoon the CO paraded the IORs in an effort to find the ringleaders, ordered them to be marched and doubled (that is, made to run). This continued for 100 minutes by which time some were ready to drop from sheer exhaustion. A few fainted and British personnel who rushed to their assistance were ordered to leave them alone.

One man was allegedly kicked by the CO and others were denied medical assistance. Finally the Indians refused point blank to run any more. This led to a verbal battle with our officers swearing and being sworn at.

Next day the hunger strike continued. The IORs then made the decision not to report for duty the following day, 6 January. They were now technically mutineers. At this point, weakened by over two days fasting, the Indians took to resting on their charpoys. But passive resistance was met by brute military force when several lorry loads of Madras Grenadiers (Indians) appeared on the scene. To our amazement and my dismay, some 200-300 soldiers armed with rifles infiltrated past our billets and towards those of the Indians. What happened at their billets I never heard, but the IORs were marched to a site away from the main camp and guarded closely.

That evening twenty or so British airmen were on patrol looking for Indian stragglers who may have escaped the net and this search continued through the night. To my relief I was not involved, my sympathies being with the mutineers, racial discrimination having sparked off the whole sorry affair.

The Indians sent details of their grievances to the newspapers. I feared more trouble and being involved in some military action against the IORs, though to refuse to do so would have meant being court-martialled. From the authorities point of view, with Indians desiring independence and repeatedly in the throes of communal violence, the last thing needed was an incident that was British officer-inspired.

RAF Tambaram 1947.
Jack and Lewis on right of the photo; others forgotten.

The following day at the airfield our Indian wireless-operators were replaced by British wireless-operators imported for the occasion. Unable at the end of my duty to find a lorry I walked across the paddy fields and met two of the mutineers, Chatterji and Bhattacharya (both of whom I knew well). They had been allowed out of detention for a few minutes to pick up clean clothing. Both seemed in good spirits and determined not to return to work.

Our CO called a so-titled welfare meeting to address his RAF airmen. He expressed his feelings towards the IORs and apologised to us for the fact that 'our dusky brethren' (his exact words) had caused so much trouble. He also promised us almost anything, short of immediate repatriation.

Mid-afternoon an Avro Anson arrived with Group Captain Bristow on board. We guessed he had come to deal with the mutiny and this was indeed the case.

On 8 January I was on morning duty and at 09.00 Group Captain Bristow took off in the Anson. He had advised the Indians to return to work, then he would thoroughly investigate their grievances. This satisfied them, they resumed duties, but remained under open arrest and eventually there would be an official Court of Enquiry.

Some of the Indians were sick and had been transferred to the Central Military Hospital. The Central Military Hospital was situated near the Bay of Bengal and I was detailed to guard these Indians and on arrival was detailed to do a 16.00 - 18.00 hrs. guard duty.

9 January was my 21st birthday and I spent my coming of age, then 21 not 18 as now, patrolling from 02.00 - 04.00 hrs. I felt a complete fool armed with my rifle and fixed bayonet. Further duties were 12.00 - 14.00 and 22.00 - 24.00. What a birthday! Five of us were guarding five sick Indians. This was so ridiculous that I propped my rifle against the wall and chatted to the prisoners. One of my 'comrades' came on duty to relieve me, but found me sitting on a chair having a political discussion. He immediately threatened to report me to the CO.

The hospital was a large one situated only a hundred metres or so from the sea from which blew a cooling breeze. The docks were in view and a large cargo vessel from the USA was being unloaded.

The wards were long, straw-thatched huts each containing about forty beds. Outside the wards the sand was filthy, littered with orange peel, soiled cotton wool and other rubbish. Our meals we took with British nursing orderlies, not good meals either.

The previous day our orders had been to report for guard duty bringing only bedding and toiletries, no mention of a change of clothing. By the end of the second day my clothes were filthy.

The third day we were even grubbier, so we asked a corporal of the station police when five new guards would be sent to relieve us, and received an unsatisfactory answer. So I phoned up one of the officers and asked if he could help, which he did. I did a morning 08.00 - 10.00 guard, but spent the afternoon duty in the ward talking to my 'prisoners' and sharing their chapattis and drinking tea. Soon after an ambulance arrived to take me back to camp to return to my met. duties. I was about to enter the ambulance when the young AC2 who had threatened to report me popped up to ask me whose permission I had to leave. Normally in control, on this occasion I was furious and gave him a flow of invective, threatening dire consequences for his neck if he persisted in pestering me. That evening I called upon my three Bengali friends, now back in their own billet, and found their company both sensible and entertaining.

All was peaceful at Vizag, the IORs back at work and being treated decently by the CO. One of the rooms in our canteen had been converted into a room for recreational use by the Indians. They of course had separate accommodation for sleeping, eating and recreation. As for the AC2 with whom I had words, I was told by a third party that he did in fact report me to the CO who took no action and I heard no more of it.

On 16 January I recorded:

> 'We now have _two_ aircraft on the airfield, a Harvard and a
> Spitfire which is the most we have seen for months! Both
> were flown here for the Court of Enquiry taking place into
> the RIAF Mutiny.

The Spitfire pilot was a Wing-Commander conducting the investigation, during which some sixty Indian airmen testified that the CO had in fact struck an Indian. Whatever the circumstances this was one thing no officer was allowed to do. Verbal abuse yes, but not physical. The Court of Enquiry must have shown sympathy to the mutineers since to my knowledge no action was taken against them.

It was said that some of the officers would be losing rank and the CO would be posted elsewhere. He was a good man in many respects, but race was his blind spot and he had handled it all rather badly. Their exact fate we never did hear. Anyway I was soon to leave.

CHAPTER 37

Tambaram - Good Food, Little Work, but Oh the 'Bull'!

In mid-January we heard that the 732 FC move to RAF Tambaram was imminent and we would be installed there by 1 February. This was all part of the general closing of RAF units and the handing over of some of our aerodromes to the RIAF, civil airlines, or in some cases just leaving them to nature. We had already been joined at Vizag by airmen from the disbanded radar stations at Cocanada and Puri.

We began the process of dismantling and crating all the meteorological equipment, the one problem being the Stevenson Screen which was embedded in six inches of concrete.

At the time, a flight lieutenant from Air Headquarters (India) arrived and admitted we were being moved to Tambaram to be 'out of the way'. There was little for us to do anywhere else. Apparently, there was also little work to be done at Tambaram either, and our stay there might be brief.

The sensible thing would have been to disband 732 FC and post us somewhere where we <u>were</u> needed, thus releasing personnel elsewhere for repatriation or demob. As it was we were already seven demob groups behind many trades.

Met. personnel in Indian now consisted of only 75 airmen with a Wing-Commander in charge. We were convinced, erroneously in all probability, that the Wing Commander was keeping us in India merely to justify his rank. When questioned about the military necessity of our Tambaram move he could only state that it would not 'do you any harm'.

My 1947 diary now had a circle round the date 2 November which was the date on which my two-and-a-half year tour ended. I ticked off the days and knew exactly how many days I still had to do. How on earth did soldiers pre-1939 stand several years in India?

I had completed nine-and-a-half months at Vizag, but was short of the twelve month maximum the reward for which was a posting to a cooler aerodrome. That was now impossible, so in a sense I had jumped climatically from the Madras St Thomas Mount frying pan into the Vizagapatam fire, only to go back to the Madras Tambaram frying pan.

On 29 January the three of us (Lewis, Dennis and me) were up early, transport taking us to the airfield to load up our equipment, back to camp for the five IOR wireless-operators and our own personal kit, then on to Waltair railway station. Other Indian airmen crowded onto the lorry to give their countrymen a good send-off.

Our train was a military special, the compartment too filthy to sit in without dusting it down. On the positive side eight of us had a whole carriage to ourselves. Military specials were usually less crowded, but now of course there were less British servicemen in India, so many having returned to the UK. We were becoming an endangered species.

The cooks had plentifully supplied us with food issuing 2lb of tomatoes, a tin of butter and thirty hard-boiled eggs each costing the equivalent of 1p each. Tomatoes were 7½p a pound, not cheap in those days.

We had a poor night's sleep, waking at each stop, when our bedding was pitched onto the filthy floor. At Madras Central an RAF lorry took us to Tambaram where we dumped our equipment inside the empty Flying Control building, then found temporary quarters. The billets at least had electric lights and each of us had a kit locker. Even the beds were superior to the usual charpoys.

The Airmen's Mess was a surprise. It had electric fans and lighting, there were drinking glasses and Indian bearers took away the empty plates. The food prepared by a civilian contractor, was the best I had eaten at any unit in India. It was of good quality and given in man-sized portions. It was a dream. We even had coffee for breakfast, as well as cornflakes and bananas. The main meal on 3 February was soup, followed by roast beef, baked potatoes and Yorkshire pudding, then a doughnut.

I had been told that Tambaram was one of the best RAF stations in India. The food and billets bore this out, but my informant also warned 'one of the most disciplined'.

That it was an ex-naval station, was evident in the Control building. This consisted of thirty large rooms, all empty - no electric light fittings, no telephone or furniture. Communication between rooms could be made naval style by using a speaking tube with which we had some fun. Signs had been left over each door, such as 'ratings lavatory', 'WRN's lavatory' etc. We chose two rooms for our Met. Office.

Whereas Vizag had no hangars, Tambaram had several. We were told that no aeroplanes had landed for twelve months. The runways were well silted and partially covered by derelict ex-naval lorries - over 200 of them! Eventually the runways were swept clean by hordes of Indian sweepers, mainly poor little women using hand brushes. They bent forward, one hand on the brush, the other hand behind the back, sweeping the silt into tiny piles, not easy as the sea breezes disturbed their efforts. Talk about labour-intensive.

The airmen's billets were in straight lines, made of brick with red tiled roofs. The camp's characteristic colour, including the sandy soil, seemed to be red. There was accommodation for one thousand personnel, but we had a mere hundred. The downside to the place would be the discipline. As soon as we arrived the Station Warrant Officer mentioned the word 'parades' and my heart sank as he handed us red eagles to be sewn onto bush shirts.

There was a working parade at 07.00. After one such we were marched to Station Sick Quarters for an FFI, the first in my case for months. Not since Skegness had I been marched to Station Sick Quarters. There were CO's parades, pay parades, Saturday morning billet inspections and guard duties. On these wretched parades we were expected to look smart, yet it was virtually impossible to obtain new clothing.

I visited stores to rid myself of three threadbare sheets and a pair of worn-out physical training shoes. One man had tried for two years to obtain a decent pair of shoes. We found that the stores had no sheets, shoes, socks or shorts. Yet on the next parade we would be criticised for wearing worn, scruffy clothing.

On one work parade an officer poked me in the back and simply said 'Haircut'. Only six days previously I had had one. The reward for non-compliance was an extra guard, so I decided on a weekly haircut.

On parades I amused myself watching the efforts of officers and NCOs to look inflatedly important, vying with each other. One unpleasant aspect was having to stand motionless whilst the sweat trickled down one's body, being tormented at the same time by flies. To move was to incur the wrath of the SWO.

One NCO, who often took morning parade, was a smallish man with large feet. Some of the lads contacted Radio SEAC (South East Asia Command)

and one evening we heard:

'Dedicated to Flight Sergeant J.......... of RAF Tambaram the following record 'His Feet's Too Big'. We looked forward to next day's parade.

One military event I did enjoy was the appearance of the 6th Warwick Regiment who on 3 February gave a fine concert of popular pieces. I am firmly of the opinion that military bands are the best thing to come out of the fighting forces.

It was probably at Tambaram, though possibly at Palam my next aerodrome, that the RAF named roads after prominent officers from the RAF's history. These were signposted, but one night a brave humorist (or humorists) changed the word Trenchard into Pilchard, Salmond lost the 'd' to become Salmon. There were other equally fishy offerings which I cannot remember. Also Gossage had been changed to Sausage. It caused much amusement next day.

During February 1947 we did not do one hour of meteorological work. Most days we just reported to the office where, although we now had electric power and a telephone, we were without any furniture. This was ridiculous and convinced me even more strongly that at Tambaram we were just wasting our time. One day I asked Flying Officer Ramamurthy, rather with tongue in cheek, if he thought there was any danger of us doing any work in the next few weeks. Fortunately he could take a joke. Truth to tell I was leading such an easy life that I had grown out of the work ethic, Protestant or otherwise.

This being 'winter' the temperature was about bearable. The aerodrome was in a better geographical position than Vizag. There our huts had been rather shut in by trees and hills. Here we were about 90ft (27m) above sea level, but even this slight elevation helped us catch some of the breeze blowing in from the sea.

On 28 February we had a visit from Flight Lt. Reynolds of No. 2 (India) Group. He gave us little positive information, but did suggest two of us would be posted from Tambaram pretty soon. We had once been told we were to become an important forecast centre, but now it seemed that when we started work, assuming we ever did, that our laboriously plotted weather charts would only be used for instructional purposes and not for flying personnel.

Dennis and I, wishing to further question Flight Lt. Reynolds, stopped him just before his Avro Anson was about to take-off. He could tell us little more. Even I, mechanically disadvantaged as I was, knew enough about aircraft to realise his 'Annie' looked on its last legs. I thought 'better you in that crate than me, chum'.

In the absence of work I engaged myself in learning German, reading, resting and visiting the splendid canteen. This was a huge building some 70 yds. (64m) long. Here amongst other things we could buy ice-cream and iced drinks. What an easy life this was, but how militarily pointless. Not being gainfully employed we kept a low profile and the three of us avoided being in the billet for the CO's Saturday inspections.

By early March the aerodrome was again operational and we even had air activity, principally the ubiquitous Dakotas, the old twin-engined workhorses of Transport Command. Being now fully equipped with wireless sets, plus operators -and furniture! - we began work again on 1 March. The 'skive' was over. The work consisted of morning or afternoon duties. Our corporal confined himself to morning only, the coolest time of the day. I challenged him on this, not too graciously, and he agreed to put himself on the duty roster.

With the runways in use we were unable to take short cuts across the airfield when on duty. Our billet was on the opposite side of the airfield to Flying Control. The airfield covered a vast area and the detour meant a two mile walk each way. A year before we arrived the aerodrome had been used by the Royal Naval Air Service.

One incident on duty sticks in my mind. One of Ramamurthy's fellow officers was a pilot. On this particular morning the Indian was flying a Harvard, a single-engined American 'plane largely used as a trainer. He decided to show his flying skill by 'shooting-up' the Control Tower a few times. This meant flying straight at us, almost at ground level, then pulling up in the last few seconds. Of course he missed the building, but not by much. To me this was

Bhattacharya,
Wireless Operator RIAF.

162

undisciplined flying at its worst. Little Ramamurthy seemed unconcerned and failed to understand 'Lowday' being so annoyed. I had no wish to end my life due to the cockiness of an exhibitionist flyer, Indian or otherwise.

Now that we were no longer unemployed and that we were now shift workers, those in authority agreed that our presence was no longer needed for morning work and colour-hoisting parades. I had no regrets at not being ordered around on a parade ground. Meteorology I enjoyed, but the rest of it was never for me.

CHAPTER 38
'Guarding' RAF Tambaram

At Tambaram fifteen of us were needed each night for guard duties, thus we were involved once every fortnight or so. Each duty had a certain character of its own. The first, on the night 18/19 February, saw us wearing ceremonial belts and carrying rifles. Dead on 18.00 hrs. we marched to the foot of the flagstaff to lower the RAF flag. Our little Flying Officer Ramamurthy was officer-in-charge, but made something of a pig's ear of it ordering us to perform some impossible manoeuvres with our rifles. The flag lowered, we marched to our various posts, mine being the Station Armoury where I stood from 22.00 - 01.00, trying to ward off sleep with an occasional walk. It was a starry night and the Plough, Pleiades and Orion were distinct. My brother was a keen astronomer and I wondered if, separated by thousands of miles, he was doing an early evening sky search. After a sleep in the Station Guardroom I was roused at 04.30 for a two hour stint. It all sounds tedious and it was.

6/7 March was my second duty, also at the armoury. During the night I managed a well-deserved dressing down from a Warrant Officer. He caught me 'guarding' the armoury with hands in pockets, talking to a fellow airman. A few minutes earlier I would have been caught sitting on a box, leaning against the armoury wall. I was told that people had been shot for such behaviour.

My attitude was one of awkward hostility to RAF procedures as laid down in KR's (King's Regulations). I had never read, or even seen the book which was a manual of how things should be done in the RAF. It allegedly contained some anachronisms. One, probably apocryphal, was that an airman had to sleep so many yards from his horse.

My third guard on 20/21 March:

> *'An eerie guard it proved to be. With Jacobs I guarded*

stores, a collection of buildings containing numerous articles of clothing, equipment etc. It was dark and mysterious down there since the stores are situated over three-quarters of a mile from any inhabited buildings.

Every so often the trees rustled and the jackals howled in the distance. Jacobs told me that on the very spot we were standing had been a burial ground. He also told me one night he himself was frightened by two stones falling near his feet.

By this time I was beginning to get quite nervy and began looking out of the corner of my eyes for all kinds of mysterious creatures - none came of course! To crown everything, a door was given quite a hard knock by someone or something - certainly not by the wind, because it was by then dead calm. What the noise was made by I don't know, but Jacobs and I picked up our rifles and advanced in the direction from which the sound came. Strange to say no one was there, although possibly it could have been a thief who made off quickly in the darkness. None of the locks had been tampered with'.

Someone had given a very heavy door quite a rattling, but it remained a mystery, fed by nervousness and the stories of my Indian companion. The replacement guard came, to my relief. Once back in my billet I read a letter from my mother saying that my brother, Raymond, then thirteen, was ill suffering from a form of food poisoning.

The 4/5 April duty was at Station Headquarters, passing uneventfully, with no bumps in the night.

A few days previously, 1 April, was a special day for the RAF being the 29th Anniversary of its formation. I wondered if there was any significance in the All Fool's Day date. I felt that we were the fools caught in the peace-time RAF. To celebrate we had a parade, no less, after which the rest of the day was free, though not for me, being on duty. It was too hot to work with the temperature 89°F at 16.10.

On 14/15 April my guard commander was an ex-124 Squadron Sergeant who was stationed at Coltishall whilst I was there. This time I was ordered to the main gate which meant checking the passes of all civilian employees arriving for work at the aerodrome. In two hours, at least 300 civilians booked in. They were guards, bearers, cleaners, sweepers and other manual workers. To examine their passes I used my few words of Tamil. What a vast amount of employment we gave to lower caste Hindus and to the so-called Untouchables. Many of these poor people must have been saddened by the British leaving.

My final night's guard duty was again at the armoury. It passed uneventfully, which was what RAF life was normally like.

CHAPTER 39
Coming Independence for India

With Indian Independence now a near certainty it was apparent that the RAF in India was now being gradually wound down. On 17 March we heard that RAF Vizagapatam had closed and I wondered whether Indian civilians had taken over Basha B5, or would the wild life gradually reclaim the site. St Thomas Mount too had closed and was now being run by civil air authorities. A whole crowd of BORs and IORs had been posted, though I felt our closure was not too far off.

On 28 March I learnt that I had been posted to RAF Palam, an aerodrome a few miles from the capital, New Delhi. This would give me the chance to see something of northern India. It was now almost ten months since I had had leave in the hills. Possibly from Palam I could get to Simla. To Simla all New Delhi's officials moved lock, stock and barrel during the hot season, taking their families with them. New Delhi was hundreds of miles from the sea, colder than Madras Province in winter, but hotter though less humid in summer.

The RAF plan, which we did not know at the time, was to withdraw us all to Palam or Mauripur near Karachi. As my tour end was now only seven months off I was not too concerned where I spent it, though given a choice I would have settled for Mauripur. 'Jock' Elliot and Iain Malcolm were already there.

On 21 February 1947 we had heard the news that the Prime Minister, Mr Atlee, had announced that India would be given complete freedom by June 1948, which presumably also meant the withdrawal of all British troops. This was pleasing news. I had been suspicious of the Government's intentions. It was now clear that they were not merely carrying on Churchill's Empire politics, the latter being opposed to Indian Independence.

In spite of my moans and groans I was pleased to have been in India and to have met so many Indians. I had seen the poverty and children deprived of education, and basic health care. I had also seen poor housing, subsistence living and near starvation. I had seen it all and this was the country from which Britain annually drew £100 million in dividends, an enormous sum then.

Some days before the Atlee announcement I had received a reply from our local MP. I had asked when India was to be given independence. He could give no assurances and used the expression 'the powers that be', so even at the eleventh hour this back bencher was as much in the dark as the rest of us. This did nothing to enhance my confidence in democracy. At that time I did not realise that MPs were often so much Westminster lobby fodder, however valuable their constituency work might be.

Demobilisation still occupied our minds. Early February met. assistant demob was up to Group 49 (mine being Group 60). We were told that Group 58 would be released by the end of 1947.

Realistically I would be out in February or March 1948, but by the time I became a civilian around five million servicemen and women would already have been released. Work might not be easy to find. For a brief spell I wondered if somewhere like Sweden might be a good idea. It seemed like a paradise of democratic socialism, neutral, prosperous and with no imperial world rôle. In addition there was a Stockholm pen-friend called Margit. I made enquiries, not too whole-heartedly. It was all a bit of a fantasy.

Back in the UK the freezing weather and snow of the 46-47 winter had given the poor, war-battered Britons, a hard time. There was rationing and a shortage of coal. In the 1940s coal was the main means of 'heating' a house - or should I say heating one spot, the living room, whilst ice formed inside the bedroom windows. Were those houses cold! The coal shortage put factory workers on part-time. For years the coal mines had been neglected and industrial relations had been bitter, even during the war.

For the coal shortage the Minister of Fuel, 'Manny' Shinwell took the brunt of the blame, but a blow was dealt to the Government from which it never really recovered. The coldest winter since 1880 had brought storms, ice and snow, then floods. The transport system was totally disrupted. The country's situation was desperate, but out in India we only knew of it from letters and outdated English newspapers.

On 3 March a letter from my mother brought the sad news that her sister Alice had died. My mother, then 44, in her life had experienced the loss of baby sister Violet (9 months old), older sister Gertrude (18 years) who died in childbirth, brother Ernie (22) killed near Ypres in 1915 and May two years later aged 22.

As for Alice who lived in Liverpool, one of her little girls died in infancy and three other daughters contracted tuberculosis. One of them, Ivy, of whom I was really fond died aged 21. Only one sister, Dora, was untouched by TB. Life was hard for working-class people. My belief in socialism was not some academic fad, but based on what formed my family background.

At this time I could not accept the euphemisms concerning death. It looked to me then and still does, that death is a chance affair with no 'calling people home'. As for Christianity I was often in a whirl of uncertainty, totally confused by all that I had read, chopping and changing between belief and unbelief. Childhood faith passed as I grew older, only to be rekindled for a time in India. Now, all these years later I believe all religions are seeking after truth, but no one faith or creed has a monopoly of truth, or anywhere near it.

My Hindu friends talked of God and showed greater tolerance towards other faiths than did most Christians in 1947. My formative years had seen the cruelty of World War Two, the slaughter of the Jews in the Holocaust and now in front of my eyes was the poverty and squalor of India. I could see little justice in the world, certainly no grand plan. Some did. One officer at Vizag believed God had guided his bomber over Germany.

CHAPTER 40
Last Weeks in Southern India

On 22 March the RAF announced that in future we would be allowed money with which to buy all items of service clothing. The fifteen shillings (75p) a month was also for laundry and shoe repairs. Considering the poor quality of Indian leather this was not a generous amount. In the UK where more clothing was worn the money would have been inadequate, but this was not likely to be my problem for long.

A week later we had what we thought would be the final clothing parade. My guard duty partner, Jacobs, was in charge and I had an excellent morning's haul. This IOR regarded me with awe, solely due to the fact that I was the only BOR with whom he had ever had a discussion. Anyway, in two visits I exchanged two pairs of khaki shorts, one pair of KD slacks, two pairs of socks, two sheets, braces, with a buckshee pair of white socks thrown in.

Two months later, not surprisingly, the clothing allowance scheme was discontinued in India, though not in the UK. The reason given was that Indian-made clothing was poor value for money. The money we had paid out for shoe repairs was to be refunded, but we had to supply proof. With people being moved around this was not possible.

Once April arrived we were again in the hot season. On 17 April I recorded 97°F (36°C) at 14.00. The night had been so hot that sleeping under a mosquito net was intolerable, so we slept on the veranda.

My German studies suffered from an inability to concentrate in the relentless heat. The afternoon duty next day was exhausting with a maximum of 100.5°F. This was repeated next day but on the 20th we were up to 104.5°F (40°C). My limit of tolerance was around 100°F (38°C). Even the Indian airmen were moaning about the heat. On the 26th it was 106°F (41°C) and the sun scorched us. With the heat, came drought, and water was restricted to 05.00 - 08.00, 12.30 - 14.00 and 17.00 - 18.00. It was adequate for our needs.

The heat was appalling, but as it was a dry heat I was free of the wretched prickly heat.

My good friend Lewis who had been at Vizag with me made a lucky escape from the heat. He was flown home to attend a Civil Service interview (for met. work). I was pleased for him when he left on 2 May, though his comradeship would be missed. I also missed my Indian friend Bhattacharya. Since January he had been posted from Vizag to Nagpur, on to Lahore, finally ending up at AHQ(I) in New Delhi. He was convinced that three postings in four months was a form of punishment for being a suspected mutiny leader. He, Lewis, Jock and Iain were the best friends of my life. In the RAF people came and went. There was no permanence. One's friends were vital to one's sanity, people to confide in, people with whom to share one's hopes and fears, those who made existence bearable.

During my stay at Tambaram I made the occasional visit to Madras. When travelling by road this took me past my old aerodrome at St Thomas Mount. There would be the occasional film or a meal at my favourite Chinese restaurant, but never to eat Chinese food. Like most Britons I was conservative in that respect. Fifty years ago most of us knew nothing of non-British food, words such as chow mein, lasagne and poppadam meant nothing to us.

Whenever in Madras I bought one or two books, now having acquired far more than could be taken back on a troopship I started sending home parcels of books.

My last ever trip to Madras was on 30 April, the last time too for Lewis who was soon to leave. We had a meal together, looked through the bazaars which, like a flea market, sold almost everything. There were a few European-type shops and masses of stalls, plenty of bargains, but it was inadvisable to get carried away. The day was cooler, 96°F, the lowest for a fortnight.

At one time all the Madras canteens and restaurants would have been full of servicemen, now the canteens had closed and the restaurants were half empty. During the war there had been four RAF aerodromes near Madras, one naval aerodrome and several Army regiments. Then, of course, there were the American servicemen. Now almost all these units had closed and the personnel, in the main, had resumed their civilian lives.

In a short while India would be independent and Madras seemed full of the ghosts of the men I had known two years before. We were the last of a long line of British servicemen in the city, a place I liked, save for the heat. Happily after Partition Madras experienced little communal violence, being so predominantly Hindu.

I had now been in the RAF three years (some conscripts did six), but the war long over I found military service peacetime style barely tolerable. At 21 it was both annoying and humiliating to be constantly ordered:

'All airmen, repeat all airmen, will parade at ....'

'Disciplinary action will be taken against those failing to attend'. ....

'A concert will be enjoyed by all ranks'.

Everything in the peacetime RAF was done by order, every order backed by threats.

The organisation had its inequalities, the squadron leader's £2.45 per day was my pay for a week. At the time of course I made no allowance for his extra responsibility. I never took kindly to the imposed discipline, being too much of a critical individual to readily conform.

The system of demob remained unfair. I met a young airman who had recently arrived in India. He did not care for the climate, but was unconcerned as he was being demobbed in three months time. I had already been overseas two years longer than he had, yet he was going home simply because airmen in his trade were way in front of ours. The sheer injustice of it rankled and we nursed our grievances.

CHAPTER 41
Rail Journey to New Delhi

My posting to Palam had been delayed for six weeks awaiting the arrival of an Indian airman due to take my place. The idea of leaving southern India appealed, though I did not relish the journey of 1,361 miles (2,190km) which was the equivalent of London to Leningrad. New Delhi, however, was a comparatively modern city with plenty to offer in the way of shops and entertainment, whilst Old Delhi had buildings of great antiquity.

So on 7 May I left Tambaram at 19.00 with Dennis. We travelled by lorry to Tambaram village's railway station from where the electrified line ran to Madras Central, where we had a second class berth on a military special - very special! Our coach had squalid compartments, the electric fans were u/s (unserviceable), likewise the electric lights which shone dimly.

There were two berths either side, which at least meant there was somewhere to sleep. We had two army companions, a warrant officer and a sergeant. The latter was an amusing character who made frequent droll remarks. He had the bizarre habit of frequently cleaning his shoes and polishing his buttons. Already an Oxford graduate he was in the Royal Army Educational Corps, destined to become a Church of England minister. His parishioners were in for some truly hilarious sermons.

At 21.20 heading towards Bezwada I took my last look at Madras, another chapter closed. Next day was hot and dirty; because of the intense heat we had to keep the windows open. Looking at the countryside one saw a hot, inhospitable landscape, with some arable land growing rice and pasture that looked dried up. The villages looked dusty and poverty-stricken. One village had a row of houses facing the railway line. Outside was strewn all the families' refuse; the wandering cows were skinny. A few chickens and a scraggy-looking dog completed this fleeting glimpse of wretched, grinding poverty.

At every station there were the pleading beggars. The poverty to be found in that vast population was overwhelming. In contrast, we lived in comparative luxury. For the journey we had been well-supplied with tinned corned beef, salmon, fruit and baked beans. No bread - instead we had packets of those incredible tooth-breaking biscuits, square and rock hard.

All through the day the sergeant kept us amused with his flow of humorous remarks. The night was exceptionally hot and my RAF issue waterbottle contained only tepid water. I kept thinking of our well at home from which we pumped really cold water. Oh for a couple of glasses of it. Luckily we had a storm during the night. The heavy rain and rushing winds cooled the atmosphere and, for once, gave me sound sleep, never easy on an Indian train.

9 May, the third day on the train. We looked out at the passing scene, much the same as in southern India, the same poverty-stricken villages, the same flat monotony with a surprising amount of agriculturally valueless land, covered in rocks and supporting little vegetation, except for stunted bushes. There were the usual fields of rice, but the dates hanging in yellowy-orange bunches I had never seen before. If anything the country was less green than in Southern India. The English countryside was incomparable, so beautifully verdant as I now realised. Never again would I take if for granted.

Next day we reached Agra, journey's end for Dennis. In the distance was the Taj Mahal which I profoundly regret not having seen at close quarters. My excuse was the heat, which led to lethargy, but what a missed opportunity.

Now in the north of the country I could see differences. The people's skins were less dark, some of the women, Muslims, wore veils, we saw camels and less oxen and bullocks. As a child I associated India with elephants, tigers and monkeys. Monkeys I had seen on the present journey, but no elephants or tigers. The nearest I ever got to a tiger was a picnic spot in the Nilgiris which 'Ma' Weston said was the occasional haunt of a tiger.

As we neared Delhi the country became ever drier and the stirred-up dust affected visibility which was surprisingly poor.

The train was several hours late which prolonged the discomfort, but mattered little otherwise. As Delhi came in sight that familiar apprehensive feeling registered in the pit of the stomach - concern about the unknown no doubt.

Here I was in Delhi. It was 10.45 and sixty-two and a quarter hours since leaving Madras. I was hot and thirsty, looking and feeling filthy. Palam was

174

several miles away. The RAF seemed reluctant to send transport, but after four long hours a vehicle turned up. By this time I was as filthy in temper as in body. On such occasions I had a low patience threshold, being on a short fuse.

CHAPTER 42
RAF Palam and VIPs

Once at Palam there was the usual booking-in, but on my rounds I found most sections friendly and helpful, with none of the awkward, obstructionist types one occasionally met. There were many familiar faces, some ex-Vizag and, surprisingly, an ex-Hamond's School lad, Kenneth Moore, who had been a classmate. He gave news of another of our schoolfellows there which was unusual since it was such a small grammar school with, pre-war, only 120 on roll. Of that number on the 1938 school group photo eight had been killed, mainly aircrew. Ten others who had been at the school before my time were also killed. A fund was set up as a memorial to their memory.

The billets, solidly built of stone had an unaccustomed luxury, fans. One with blades almost of aircraft propeller size whirred away over my bed. The billets kept surprisingly cool. All doors and windows were kept closed to exclude the hot air and the persistent dust.

The lads in the billet seemed a good crowd though I never formed any close friendships. Often we were too tired to be sociable. The billet lacked comfortable chairs so, when reading I took to my bed, usually falling asleep, waking up half dazed.

Two airmen from Yelahanka were posted to us. They eventually arrived bringing their gramophone and pile of swing records with which we became all too familiar. The gramophone duo within a couple of days were driving us crazy playing the records incessantly. Such was communal life.

In our billet we had a Jewish airman. One day two of our room-mates were holding forth airing their anti-semitic prejudices. When they had finished holding court, our Jewish friend quietly and gently revealed his identity. From the two by way of apology came the inevitable:

'Oh, but you're different'.

The Airmen's Mess food was tolerable, but nothing near as good as at Tambaram where, because there was no need to supplement the RAF diet, I was able to save money. Here I again needed the canteen, which was tastefully decorated in green with new writing desks fitted with reading lamps. There were easy chairs, carpets and curtains; luxury indeed.

The Educational and Vocational Section was a well-equipped building with a helpful staff. There was a good supply of books and a weekly music appreciation group using the usual portable gramophone.

The cinema was the best RAF cinema I had seen since Cardington. There was a change of programme each evening and I frequently attended when off-duty. The one drawback was the cigarette smoke which caused aching, stinging eyes. The atmosphere reeked since most smoked. At Vizag we had even been supplied with free tins of fifty. Never having had the habit mine were given away. Was the free issue to encourage the lads to smoke? As if.

Being the main airport for New Delhi, with its Government buildings, civil servants and high-ranking military personnel, RAF Palam was a busy aerodrome. This necessitated 24 hour cover in the Met. Office. We did one night duty in five, but we were excused all guard duties and most parades. Certainly the steady stream of aeroplanes meant real work that mattered and I would be unlikely to be posted elsewhere. There was nowhere to go except Mauripur - or home.

My first met. duty was on 13 May. A mass of data poured in and it was a race against time to cope with it. Any number of aircraft flew in. As well as Dakotas there were Bristol Airfreighters, Tudors, Vikings and, most interesting of all, three-engined Junkers 52s. This type had been used by the Luftwaffe as troop transports, but now they had French markings.

Many of these 'planes were operated by civil airlines and this had been one of the grouses of the RAF strikers who regarded themselves as cheap labour maintaining non-RAF aircraft.

Visibility at Palam was sometimes reduced by clouds of loose sandy soil. It blinded the eyes, covered everything in a layer of dust and entered our mouths. Even after cleaning one's teeth some grit remained. From the Control Tower it was fascinating to watch 'dust devils' making their way across the airfield. These were small vortices of spiralling sand, miniature versions of a tornado. As they touched ground I speculated on what it would be like underneath one.

On 25 May I wrote:

> *'We had the American Ambassador to India in the Met.*
> *Office. He is flying in a Fortress from Delhi to Bangkok*
> *and they are flying over the Himalayas as he hopes to see*
> *Mount Everest. Funnily enough, I saw him a few days ago*
> *on a newsreel.*
>
> *He walked in with the Yankee aircrew and didn't put on any*
> *airs and graces as a British Ambassador would. If he had*
> *been British he would have been attended by a whole*
> *crowd of army officers. This chap is the first American*
> *Ambassador to India and only arrived recently.'*

Fifty years on the US Embassy in London searched their archives and came up with the information that the Ambassador had been Henry S Grady appointed on 10 April 1947.

31 May:

> *'Field-Marshall Auchinlech arrived by Dakota.*
> *Mountbatten was there to meet him accompanied by a*
> *crowd of officers and satellites'.*

Field-Marshall Sir Claude Auchinlech, nicknamed 'the Auch', was India's Commander-in-Chief, whilst Rear-Admiral Viscount Louis Mountbatten had been appointed Viceroy on 24 March.

Ten car loads of officers had come to meet Auchinlech. But when it was announced that Field-Marshall Montgomery would be calling at Palam on his way to meet the American General Macarthur I wondered if even more car loads of officers would be dancing attendance. There was to be a full-blown RAF ceremonial parade which, at the time, I was thankful to have escaped, but looking back it would have been interesting to have been inspected by the famous 'Monty'.

I hasten to add that I did not meet any of these illustrious gentlemen. One of our airmen, however, did have a cousin who worked at Viceregal Lodge. He described a building more like a palace. The occupants seemed to live off the fat of the land, best of food and drink, air-conditioned rooms and innumerable servants. Even some of the middle-rank officers had several servants. All this a mere eight miles from our Airmen's Mess with its everlasting corned beef and baked beans. It seemed that whatever government was in power those at the top retained their high standard of living. No change there.

178

On one occasion Lord Louis gave a dinner to which he invited older RAF personnel who had served in Burma when he was in command of South East Asia forces. Sometimes these invitations were given by the great and the good in India.

'Jock' once attended a select coffee morning and, like me, never having seen real coffee cups before, came back talking of chota (small) cups and wee cakes. I have a vague recollection of once having the chance to take tea with other airmen at the home of Lord Wavell's sister I believe it was. Typically I did not go. In retrospect this was a mistake. My horizons were limited.

The summer at Palam had to be endured to be believed and even fifty years later, in 1997, Indian weather experts were comparing temperatures to those of 1947.

Being on night duty 16/17 May I arrived for work at 24.00 to find a temperature of 100°F (38°C). During the previous day it had risen from 100°F at 11.00 to 115°F (46°C) at 14.00, the hottest day I had experienced. We sweated buckets that night shift. There were five successive days when the maximum temperature reached 115°. Fortunately, being so far from the sea, it was a relatively dry heat.

The sun had to be treated with the greatest respect. It was a killer. Indians were dying in the streets of Delhi and during the previous summer three airmen had succumbed to heat exhaustion at Palam. I led a relaxed life as far as possible, perhaps seeing less of the Delhi area than I might have, but avoided sunstroke and heat-stroke. But I do regret not having made the journey to Agra to see the Taj Mahal.

The local papers told how Radio Delhi was having problems with their shellac 78 records. They were warping in the heat. No wonder I found it too hot and debilitating for sight-seeing. The heat of course produced prickly heat on my chest, but I certainly was not being overworked since we now had nine met. assistants. The duty roster was arranged so that periodically we had four-day spells off duty. We had surplus personnel in India, yet in the UK five hundred civilian met. assistants were needed.

I made an occasional visit to New Delhi, far cleaner than most cities, with many buildings of modern design laid out in geometric patterns. The general air of order and tidiness was in contrast to that of Old Dehli. New Delhi had some splendid shops and Connaught Circus, a circular shopping area, was architecturally impressive. Prices there were dearer than in the UK - apples 22½p per pound, oranges 2½p each. In neighbouring Old Delhi the same could be bought for half the price. But in New Delhi there were officials willing and able to pay inflated prices; not LACs however.

CHAPTER 43
Victors and Vanquished

The British Government endured a tough passage during early 1947. On 30 May I wrote:

'The Labour Government seems struggling amidst a shoal of difficulties and I'm afraid the combined effects of housing shortages, food scarcity, labour strikes, coal shortages etc. will ruin their chances of winning the next election. I don't blame the Government to any extent. They have been the victim of bad blows such as the 'freeze up' and the floods. No other party would have done any better, certainly not the Tories. The Government is genuinely trying to improve the life of the average citizen, but due to circumstances our standard of living will not improve for at least three years, by which time another election will be in full swing, and even if the Labour Party gets back into power it will be with a reduced majority.'

The 1950 election was won, but defeat in 1951 saw Churchill again as PM.

The war had exhausted our country. With the exception of Germany and members of the Commonwealth no other nation had fought for six years.

Of the ordinary Germans many had been dazzled by and gone along with the early years of success, others had been reluctantly netted by an all-embracing evil system. Now all paid the price of collective guilt. The mass of Germans existed on food rations marginally above starvation level. But this of course did not apply to thousands of ex-Nazi officials useful to the allies, or to V-2 scientists such as Von Braun in the USA.

Thousands of German POWs failed to return from captivity in the USSR. The latter treated their own prisoners with barbarity, whilst the German inhumanity towards Russian POWs is well documented. Not publicised was the demise of thousands of German POWs who succumbed to malnutrition and/or disease whilst captives of the USA and France. The 400,000 German POWs in the UK were the lucky ones, in the main treated well, though sometimes viewed with suspicion. Many of us simply regarded the POWs as young men, who, like ourselves, had been caught up in a war not of our making.

One problem the Government faced was maintaining sufficient service personnel. The majority of us would not be 'signing on' so National Service was to be introduced. The big debate was would it be twelve months or eighteen. In the event it was two years, but having already been in the RAF for three-and-a half years to me it all seemed rather academic.

Regarding UK food it is incredible to think we actually sent home food parcels. We paid an organisation of some kind that supplied the food which we parcelled up and posted. As an example in March I sent three 2 lb tins of peaches and one tin of pears. As we were allowed to send only one tin of fruit I re-labelled three as meat, peas and carrots! Sometimes we merely paid the money and others as did the dispatching. Food for the victors of World War Two!

CHAPTER 44

Independence Near - But Normal Life at Palam

On 3 June 1947 Viceroy Mountbatten, Jawaharla Nehru, Mohammad Ali Jinnah and Baldev Singh announced on All-India Radio that India was to be given independence and that Mr Jinnah was to have his Pakistan and that India was to be partitioned. We knew nothing of this at first, but when we did hear the news we were truly delighted. It was the beginning of the end - roll on the boat!

At a news conference the Viceroy announced that the transfer date was to be 15 August, the second anniversary of the day when as Supreme Commander SEAC, our top man, he had accepted the Japanese surrender.

To Indian astrologers the date, 15 August, was deemed not to be propitious and dire consequences, including massacres, were foretold. Even in the weeks leading up to the joint declaration communal violence with beatings, stabbings and shootings had taken place, though Delhi was quiet. In retrospect the handover was done too swiftly, dangerously so. Indians were now pre-occupied with each other and little hostility was directed against we British, but it was not to be until 28 February 1948 that the last British soldier left India. Most of us, however, would soon be going home and the 'Jewel in the Crown' no longer ours.

One evening I met Bhattacharya in Connaught Circus and over cold drinks in a restaurant we discussed religion, racism, politics and books, later adjourning to a park. Midnight soon arrived. Even though there were so many British servicemen in India it was not a common sight to see BORs and IORs socialising. Sometimes it led to looks of surprise. To an ardent Indian nationalist did his fellow-countryman appear as a collaborator?

Some Indian airman told me I was the only BOR who had ever freely chatted with them and their only lengthy conversations were otherwise to do with work.

At this time of course many British people did genuinely think whites were in some way intellectually superior to those with a brown skin. There was a wariness, reinforced by the Indians having different social customs. Our fellows saw Indian peasants eating rice with their fingers from an improvised 'plate' made of large leaves that had been sewn together. Some of our number were convinced that Indians were physically dirty. I used to point out that these poor people were not responsible for the appalling sanitation. Even the most destitute could be seen pouring cans of water over themselves and cleaning their teeth with frayed sticks.

But Indians, unlike Britons, had little idea of orderly queuing. I once joined a post office queue in Madras. The column grew ever longer thanks to infiltrators and the counter became ever more distant.

Our servicemen took exception to the sight at railway stations of Indian women struggling with cases on their heads whilst the menfolk carried rather less. Then of course some traders were downright dishonest. There was filth evident in the streets, the roads and pavements spattered with red blobs of betel-nut juice. But the discarded cans, cigarette ends and squashed chewing-gum that befoul our end of the century British streets are no less disgusting. Whatever the differences in culture there was not much effort to understand India or Indians on the part of many RAF airmen. Those of us who did make the attempt were the exceptions. I believe the majority in 1947 were just indifferent.

Only three days before the announcement of the date of independence 18-year-old airmen were still arriving from the UK. The occupants of five beds near mine had between them a total overseas service of ten months. Of the fifteen in my billet I had the second lowest demob number.

During June life in the Met. Office carried on fairly uneventfully. All the Indian wireless-operators had been posted elsewhere so British W/ops kept the channels of communication open. One night one of the heavy, bulky wireless sets managed to go absent without leave. One of our met. assistants got part of the blame. Quite how it happened we never found out. Perhaps he had dozed off and a loose-wallah (thief) managed to take it. But where was the wireless operator? I had known wireless-operators fall asleep at their sets. This incident led to all of us receiving a pep talk on the subject of slackness and indiscipline.

One night I was on duty with 'Jet' the sergeant. We were both dead tired by dawn, when a group captain walked into the office. We failed to jump to attention. The verbal flak that followed was mainly directed at our sergeant, the penalty for having three stripes.

In my diary I wrote:

> *'A stupidly pompous little s....... glorying in his power and brimful of arrogance.'*

Our workload was reduced. We now plotted weather charts at only 08.00 and 17.00. Previously we did five a day. To reach Flying Control more speedily we were able to use cycles.

The climate during June remained unpleasantly hot and the food everlastingly monotonous, with plenty of corned beef, baked beans and dry bread. To their credit, for several days the cooks tried their best to produce a little loaf for each of us. This was a tall order, there being about 500 of us. The last batch of loaves were fine, but the earlier ones were rock-hard, so the experiment came to an end.

After being missing for many months my documents at last turned up. These written records of my inglorious military career were vital since without these my eventual repatriation could have been delayed.

CHAPTER 45
Himalayan Foothills and a Dodgy Dakota

On 17 June I heard that I was one of a hundred men being sent from Palam on hill party. Thirty-two of the hundred were regulars (men who had signed on for a period of RAF service). The rest were conscripts and of those I had the lowest demob group, whereas at Coltishall I had about the highest.

Five days later we had our kit weighed for our trip to Chaklala near Rawalpindi. We were allowed 70 lb (32 kg) of kit. I must admit my first air trip filled me with some misgivings, not being unfamiliar with Dakotas and their ways.

<u>23 June</u>

> '*At 08.00 reported to the Guardroom from where we were transferred by gharry to the airfield where five Dakotas were waiting for us, one for our kit and four for us.*
>
> *I was in the second to take off - KN 691 of 10 Squadron. After a roll call we went on board at 08.30 and after a few minutes delay taxied onto the runway. Here I experienced some qualms wondering if we would leave the ground OK; and needless to say my fears were quite groundless. We soon hurtled along the runway with engines full throttle and became airborne.*
>
> *Gradually we climbed to a few thousand feet and after a few preliminary bumps had a smooth trip. The country for the most part was very brown and dusty with several score of villages surrounded by green, fertile strips of cultivated land. The only place of any size that we passed over was Lahore whose congested centre will long remain in my memory, spread out before us and reminding me of a model city and not an actual one.*
>
> *Eventually we came within sight of some barren, hilly country where we experienced some bumps due to rising air currents and the*

sensation was similar to being on a ship. With continuing bumps we came over Chaklala aerodrome and soon came down towards the strip with engines revving slowly (or so it seemed) and made a good landing, taxiing towards the parking strip where Air Transport gharries were waiting for us.

The journey to Lower Topa took three hours due to frequent breakdowns by the gharry in front of us and we wasted further time by stopping at a so-called canteen halfway up the hillside.

After tearing along precipitous roads, driven by drivers who overtook at bends, I considered myself fortunate to have reached Lower Topa at all!

We had left Palam at 09.00, arriving at Chaklala at 11.50 - 364 miles at 6,000 ft, speed 150 mph. It took longer to do the 30 miles Chaklala - Lower Topa road trip.

Lower Topa camp is situated at the top of a hill and all around us are forest-clad hills covered with pine trees. It's beautiful scenery, so green and wooded.'

24 June:

'Rose at 07.30 feeling fresh and alive for the first time for many months. It's a joy to be alive in such a place as this. The climate is

RAF Station Lower Topa in the foothills of the Himalayas.

187

pleasant and I have a hearty appetite for my meals. The food in the Mess is good, but not quite adequate and I supplement it by numerous tomato rolls from the char-wallah. Money soon goes here and the billet is plagued by char-wallahs and people selling walking-sticks, ice-cream, boiled eggs and even milk.

The scenery is superb and my most beautiful memories of India will be of this place and the Nilgiris.'

We led an idyllic life at Lower Topa. A squadron leader, the Station CO, gave us a pep talk telling us what and what not to do during our three weeks. It was all very relaxed and Squadron Leader Arden seemed a good type. Basically, providing we respected a few sensible ground rules, we were free to do as we pleased.

There were games facilities and as on most of my Indian aerodromes I was able to play table tennis. The library was good, I had the time to read several books and also watched some films at the camp cinema.

The weather was mixed. When the sun shone I took my current book to a secluded grassy spot on one of the beautiful tree covered slopes. Bathing in the sun increased my tan; there were no thoughts of skin cancer then.

On some days rain and low cloud kept us indoors. Cloud stretched from the valley to the top of our hill at which height the cloud enveloped us like a fog. It could be quite cold with the occasional thunderstorm. Once we even had hail, which I never thought to see in India.

At Lower Topa we lost all sense of time and I would willingly have spent the rest of my tour there. What lucky beggars the permanent staff were!

It was said that on a really clear day the Himalayas could be seen, though I have no remembrance of ever being able to do so. We were in the lower foothills of that vast range.

On 10 July there was a minor earthquake in our corner of the world. We experienced three tremors when the buildings really shook, accompanied by a sound like that of rushing wind. Not as frightening at that distance as the V-1s on London, but how terrifying to be at the epi-centre of a major earthquake. Ours would have been fairly low on the Richter Scale.

Whilst at Topa I visited the Vocational Advice Service which existed to help servicemen come to a decision on their future careers after demobilisation, assuming they had no career in mind or, as in my case, wished to make a complete break and start afresh. A minority had joined up straight from school. Some of course had jobs to which they wanted to return.

After a preliminary interview by a VAS sergeant it was necessary to do a series of tests in Maths, English etc. One test was basically engineering-based and with my poor track record in all things mechanical I surprised myself by obtaining a good mark. Once the result had been assessed an interview with a VAS officer was arranged.

Amongst possibilities discussed were social work, Ordnance Survey, meteorology, teaching or obtaining a place at one of the universities. For the latter I would have had to obtain a government grant in order to live. Tuition would have been free. How strange that it was then obtainable in poor war-torn Britain, but not under the present government ruling a far more affluent society.

It is interesting to reflect that the weekly pay for both met. assistants and OS workers at this time was only £4 per week whereas I as an LAC had £2.45 as virtually weekly pocket money. £4 would have been little for a married man with a family to keep. At this time I was uncertain what I would do as a civilian, but had many more months in which to decide. The VAS information and advice were helpful.

On 11 July I wrote in my diary:

> *'In the headlines today we have news of Princess Elizabeth's engagement. I used to despise royalty. I still think they are useless, but I feel sorry for them now. The King has had a struggle to overcome his speech impediment and since he hates crowds he must live a life of misery.'*

The young Princess Elizabeth in such a few years would be Queen. Nowadays I have no problem with the monarchy as such, but like most Britons respect some royals more than others.

One day a walk took me to the Sandes' Home at Chikagali, a real relic of empire where troops had relaxed for two generations. It had an evangelical air with lots of religious pamphlets spread around as well as books and magazines, including bound volumes of 'Sphere' dated 1926-27. The Indian hills had many such little British oases.

The food deteriorated towards the end of the leave and was heavily weighted in favour of - yes, corned beef and baked beans. Water too became a problem, being available until 08.00, then the taps were dry for several hours. Back in Delhi the monsoon was late and there was an acute water shortage both for agricultural and domestic use.

Three days before the end of our time one tooth was giving me trouble, my teeth not having been regularly checked, through no fault of mine. Eventually the tooth was agonisingly painful, causing my head to throb. Fourteen aspirins on the last day achieved nothing in pain alleviation. I wondered about an abscess.

15 July:

> '*Called at 04.00, handed in sheets and pillow-cases to stores, had breakfast at 05.00. By 06.00 we were waiting for transport, my tooth aching all the while and already my face beginning to swell slightly. Eventually we made our descent to Rawalpindi along treacherous, wet, slippery roads.*
>
> *It had been raining heavily for two or three hours and I began to think we would not be flying at all, but as we approached Rawalpindi the weather improved considerably and by 09.00 most of the low cloud had disappeared.*
>
> *Arrived at Chaklala to find four Dakotas waiting for us, but as one was unserviceable twenty of our fellows stayed behind. As events turned out it would have been just as well had I stayed.*
>
> *At 10.00 we took off after three preliminary false starts. Very soon after it became quite rough and I felt slightly airsick after each bump. About halfway between Chaklala and Lahore the port engine began to leak oil and eventually was stopped by the pilot, an ex-Fakenham ATC chap who became a flying officer.*
>
> *We flew on with one engine only and eventually made a one-engined landing, a piece of good work on the part of the pilot. The forced landing was at Lahore, in 1947 almost entirely an Indian Air Force aerodrome (900 10Rs and only 20 British).*
>
> *I was quite thankful to be safely on the ground again. The port engine was covered in oil, also part of the port wing. The 'false starts' to which I referred were due to a faulty starboard engine, so it had come as a shock to look out of the window to see that it was the port engine (the 'good' one!) which had its propeller feathered. So it was one engine out of action and one dodgy. The journey of just under 200 miles had taken two-and-a half hours. It was certainly eventful and potentially dangerous.*
>
> *The Dakotas then in service were old and quite a few had crashed. Some that were flying should have been grounded. Those that were flying could have been better serviced. Too many mechanics, BORs*

and IORs, were rather inexperienced.

Having landed at Lahore we decided to stay whilst the Dakota was repaired, but eventually that idea was dropped. Probably it was a lengthy major servicing that was needed or was it destined for the aircraft graveyard? An arrangement was made for another Dakota to pick us up next day, but for me it was to be otherwise.

CHAPTER 46

Hospital at Lahore and Partition Horror Ahead

<u>18 July:</u>

> '*My face swelled considerably during the night and since it was obviously an abscess I decided to report sick. Eventually after the preliminary waiting, I was sent to the Base Military Hospital at Lahore to see a dentist. He allowed me to be admitted to the BMH which is run by the Army. After the usual official waiting I was admitted to a surgical ward. Spent the afternoon reading 'The Pilot Walked Home' - perhaps he had a clapped out Dakota?*
> *At 17.30 I walked down to the operating theatre where I was given an injection of some kind which soon sent me to sleep. I woke to find myself back in bed with the aching tooth removed. It was a relief to have it out since it was beginning to make me feel quite ill. I awoke from the effects of the anaesthetic feeling rather ridiculously pleased with myself. Fortunately I kept quiet.*
> *At 21.00 I was given a penicillin injection of 2,000 units (1 cc) in the behind and I shall be having several of these during the next day. The dentist took out one tooth at the front. The swelling will gradually go down and I feel ten times better than when I came in.*'

The male nurse used to detach the end of the syringe and use it like a dart on my exposed posterior as I lay face down, being the dartboard.

There was a double purpose in initially reporting sick. Apart from the obvious one, intense pain, it enabled me to avoid flying in another grotty Dakota. As well I did not volunteer for aircrew duties.

I slept well due to the anaesthetic but was called every three hours to have my injection. These continued throughout the day, but the swelling was going down and I was feeling fine.

17 July:

> *'There are seven or eight chaps in the room and it's quite pleasant, has a radio, books, comfortable beds, fans, electric lights and is spotlessly clean. The washing facilities are quite reasonable; the food fine. To go to the lavatories we pass through an air-conditioned ward for skin patients. It's very cool in there, practically as cold as in England. The dental officer has been round to see me'.*

It was sheer delight walking through the skin ward. Next day I had my last injection, the fourteenth. At this time each penicillin jab cost 50p. I was flattered to think I was worth £7 to the RAF. The dental officer pronounced me fit for discharge on 19 July. It had been a pleasant little interlude with nothing to do except eat, sleep and read. It was also pleasing to see female English nurses, good to look at, and a change from all-male company.

I reported with my bedding to stores, being the Army it was the Quartermaster's stores. I also had to see the CO, an Army Captain, after which it was back to the aerodrome at Lahore where I spent the day feeling a little depressed, it having been an excessively hot, damp and sticky day. My clothes were not clean and were wet with perspiration. As my tin trunk had been allegedly put on a Dakota and taken back to my unit at Palam I had no clean change of clothing.

I left Lahore aerodrome at 22.00, but at the station found the next Delhi train was not until 02.00. When it did arrive what a dirty ramshackle affair with only two British on it, a sergeant and me. The sergeant kindly allowed me to borrow his greatcoat and a pillow since I was without any bedding.

The train was painfully slow, stopping every few minutes for no apparent reason, the only passengers being troops. Because of the intense heat it was necessary to keep the windows open, thereby allowing small fragments of coal, dust, soil and miscellaneous material to blow into the compartment. Each stop meant an invasion of flies.

The carriage had wooden seats and there was one small, filthy wash-basin without a plug. The lavatories were foul. Not a minute too soon, at 17.00, we arrived at Delhi by which time I was hot, damp, filthy and 'thoroughly cheesed' (fed up). The Motor Transport Section refused to send a vehicle so in the company of two lads returning from leave we hired a taxi to Old Delhi.

There we joined the so-called liberty gharry to Palam, made my way to the billet where one of the lads greeted me with the news:

'You're posted to the UK!' - or words to that effect.

Next day I checked the official accuracy of the posting and it was true. Three met. airmen from Palam, plus several from elsewhere, were on the same draft. It was to be quite a reunion as we had all come out on the 'Chitral'. Visited Station Sick Quarters for inoculations and a vaccination, and called at all the likely buildings to look for my elusive trunk. A corporal said it had been put on a Dakota, then taken off on someone's orders, so it must still be at Lahore.

The RAF gave me permission to take a train back to Lahore, the prospect not exactly thrilling me after the last journey. Still wearing borrowed kit I set off from Delhi Junction managing to gain a second class berth on the Frontier Mail, sharing a compartment with four Indian Army Officers. The carriage was comfortable and even the taps worked. At 21.00 with another night on a train in prospect we set off and I managed to sleep for most of the twelve hour journey. Just before reaching Lahore we mysteriously stopped a short distance from the village of Harbanspura. The other side of the village station we again halted and I looked out of the window to see what was happening. The train in front of ours had been stopped, a steel railway line and boulders having been placed across the line. Once the train halted, the workers on board had been attacked by men of another faith who had seemingly ambushed them. Eight had been murdered and twelve others wounded. Two bodies lay a few yards from us, both making a horrifying sight, being covered in bloody wounds. How could this be done in the name of religion?

The local 'Lahore Military Gazette' reported the incident, but wisely refrained from saying whether Hindus had attacked Muslims or vice-versa, or perhaps Sikhs were the attackers or victims. The paper stated that the driver had boldly removed a blockage at Moghalpura taking the train on to Harbanspura, so what exactly did happen I never found out, but being the only Englishman on the train I felt some concern.

Bombs had been thrown in Lahore the previous day, as well as outbreaks of arson and knife attacks. At Lahore's station a bomb had been thrown at a train compartment, hitting the outside of the carriage. Both the thrower and his accomplices were injured.

At Moghalpura a hand-grenade had been hurled into a compartment. An ex-serviceman promptly picked it up and threw it onto the platform killing two bystanders and injuring five. The hand-grenade thrower would have easily escaped in the crowd. Indian stations teemed with passengers who often clung onto the outside of carriages.

Once at Lahore station I was dead keen to be on my way to the aerodrome as quickly as possible. It was no place to linger. Sikhs were walking round armed for the protection of themselves and their families. Luckily an Army lorry driver going to the cantonment area gave me a lift.

Once at the aerodrome a call at SHQ concerning the missing trunk, drew a blank. A chit was offered to the effect that my kit was not at RAF Lahore, which was all very well, but the trunk included many personal items. Not satisfied it seemed better to give the search one more day, so I found a spare bed in a BOR billet.

Next day the police at the Guardroom suggested the Main Stores - and there it was. Arrangements made for my return to Delhi I caught the Frontier Mail at 20.00. I left Lahore with intense feelings of relief glad that no missile throwers were at work. We British were not a target, yet it was so easy to be involved in an incident, being in the wrong place at the wrong time.

Little did I know it, but on that station I had missed a bloodbath by just three weeks. Lahore was to become part of Pakistan, Delhi the capital of India. At midnight on 14 August 1947 India and Pakistan gained their freedom which became the signal for appalling bloodshed in the Punjab of which Lahore was a part. Trains were to arrive at Lahore full of butchered passengers. People were also killed on the platforms which were awash with blood.

The Punjab villages I had flown over became scenes of horror with hundreds of thousands of Hindus, Muslims and Sikhs on the move, only to be attacked by rival communities through which they passed. Hindus living in the new Pakistan headed for India, Muslims caught on the Indian side of the boundary fled to Pakistan. Sikhs would head for their sacred city, Amritsar. 'Ethnic cleansing' would happen on the sub-continent, though at the time, in spite of what the Nazis had done, we did not know the expression.

Before Partition the Lahore - Delhi line was one of the most heavily used in India, now by all accounts it is used daily by a few trains only. But to return to Lahore as it was before Partition. The Mail train from Lahore was absolutely full, with no free berths so I packed my kit into a compartment. The night was spent on the floor squatting on a pile of kitbags, sleeping in snatches of an hour or so. It was intensely hot and to make matters worse there was a European lady in the compartment so we couldn't strip off. We were crowded, it was hot and damp, we were filthy and covered in coal dust. Rail journeys in India were usually hell, but that night the end was in sight - ROTB (roll on the boat). The times we had said ROTB to each other!

CHAPTER 47
Farewell to India

Back at Palam again there were only a few days to prepare for my departure to Bombay (Mumbay now). Those of us being repatriated were expected at Worli Transit Camp, Bombay by 1 August.

The next few days were spent 'clearing', cycling to the various sections, parcelling books, tins of fruit and my acquired blanket for despatch home. Then on 27 July there was one final met. duty to be done which ended at midnight. Next evening I met Bhattacharya at Connaught Circus. We talked, but were both conscious of the fact that we would never see each other again. We did keep in contact by mail for several years and his nephew, a professor at Calcutta University, stayed with us in England. As for Bhattacharya we lost touch.

Altogether, fifty of us at Palam were being repatriated. Some of us had been overseas for over two years, some for just a few weeks which was bad planning and a waste of the money of British taxpayers. It beggared belief that some of these young lads had come all the way to India to do a minuscule 'tour' of four weeks! Unbelievable, but quite true.

A good piece of 'gen' was that Group 57 met. assistants would be released in October, so I correctly estimated my release as January 1948.

Pay accounts owed me one month's pay - Rs90 (£6) which would be useful at Bombay. As for Palam it was good to see the back of it. There was loads of pettiness, but little attempt to give regard to welfare issues. Standing for the National Anthem before each cinema performance mattered, but not those monotonous, mundane meals.

On 30 July we arrived at Delhi Junction only to wait three hours for the train to actually start. The fifty of us (repats, demobs and postings) were allocated an uncomfortable third-class Indian-style carriage with low toilets on which one squatted on one's haunches. Food, of a kind, was provided i.e.

hard biscuits and other barely edible items. I just could not face it so I lashed out, spending part of my Rs30 in the restaurant-car to buy a couple of decent meals.

We arrived at Bombay on the 31st, the 900 mile (1,448 km) journey taking 36 hrs. For the last hundred miles we left the steam locomotive behind, this part of the line being electrified. The journey through the hilly Western Ghats would have been picturesque, but the view was spoilt by low cloud and heavy rain. We had of course the usual heat, humidity and flies, but I had enjoyed my five restaurant car meals, the best for months. They had cost me one pound which sounds ridiculously cheap, but represented three day's pay for an LAC. It was well worth it.

After the usual wait, only two hours, which was good, at Bombay Station transport took us to Worli. The bus drivers dumped us at 'F' Camp in billets each of which accommodated 140 men.

Next day we paraded at 08.00, but apart from having our paybooks checked to see that our inoculations were up to date and a visit to the armoury we did little. Worli seemed disorganised and the food as poor as any I had encountered in India. There was an acute shortage of water which for tooth cleaning and drinking came round in bowsers; this was heavily chlorinated. The tap water was suspect (typhoid) and in a leaflet it was emphasised that it could only be used for washing.

The canteen was hopeless, combining poor food with high prices. Typical of Worli were the precautions against malaria. By day they were extremely strict on anti-malaria dress regulations - socks pulled well up to the knees, sleeves rolled down on bush shirts and all buttons done up. All sensible stuff, but when it came to night-time there were no mosquito nets and no sign of overhead wiring for hanging them if there had been. Perhaps the Worli mosquitoes only operated by day and had a truce by night - unlike those in the rest of India. RAF India ways took some fathoming.

I discovered the block in which I had slept in 1945. It was deserted, a forlorn sight with a heavily leaking roof. Our 1947 billet was on the sea front, the canteen only 30m from the sea which roared as waves broke against the rocky shoreline. The promenade was similar to that of an English seaside town. Worli's was quite smart and clean. It was pleasant to be so near the sea, but it had one curious effect. We sweated so much in the damp heat that our bush shirts became soaked in sweat and had white patches.

The water situation gave cause for concern. We knew that some days before our arrival two or three RAF airmen at Worli had died of typhoid. Apart from the purified bowser water the rest was kept well away from the mouth. I had no intention so near to my repatriation to die in India, though those who had died probably felt the same.

Apart from the odd parade which was a means of disseminating information, and being caught for a 24-hour guard duty, there was little to do so two of us made a trip to the centre of Bombay for a meal.

We remained at Worli for several days, the original 8 August sailing date being postponed to the 10th. This was the monsoon season and even at Worli the sea looked rough so what would it be like a hundred miles out in the Arabian Sea?

CHAPTER 48
On the 'Franconia' Heading Homewards

9 August was to be my last day in India. During the morning we had an FFI, handed in three sheets to stores and changed any remaining Indian currency into British. In 'tin town', our nickname for Worli's ramshackle shopping area, I bought a watch for Rs40 (£3) and after an evening meal in the 'Victory Café' took a walk with two others to the sea-front. As the light faded I witnessed one of the most glorious sunsets of my life. The sky took on the colours of the rainbow. It was spectacular, beautiful and memorable.

This was the end of my days in India. As a civilian perhaps the life would have been tolerable, but as an airman facing the twin handicaps of the climate and the RAF how could I not be thankful to be leaving? I had no dislike of the Indian people and wished with all my heart that India and Pakistan might one day be prosperous democratic countries. The wealth remains unevenly spread. Democracy survives in India.

For some days we had known that the troopship waiting for us at Ballard Pier was the 'Franconia'. This was a Cunard Liner 190 metres in length with a gross tonnage of 20,158. Pre-war, for over twenty years, she had carried passengers on the Liverpool - New York service. In December 1944 the 'Franconia' was used to take POWs back to the Soviet Union. The men had been in the German Army, some as volunteers, others by compulsion. They were sailing eastwards and one moonlit evening the singing of the Russians on deck was so beautiful that many listening Britons were reduced to tears by the haunting sound. Most Russian soldiers who had surrendered to the Germans received short shrift on their return to the USSR, killed or imprisoned in most cases.

The 'Franconia' two months later served as Churchill's headquarters at the Yalta Conference. At the time we knew nothing of the 'Franconia's' history'. To us the ship meant eighteen days, then home.

After yet another FFI and another check on our inoculations, we had the thrill of walking up the gangplank. By 14.00 the famous 'Gateway of India', erected in 1911 to commemorate the arrival of King George V and Queen Mary for the great Delhi Durbar, receded into the distance. Sighs of relief!

Two hours out at sea it became rough. During the evening, crowds of lads were hanging over the deck handrails, ejecting their dinners into the sea. Apart from a slightly dizzy feeling I sensed no feeling of nausea.

Down below deck we were to eat and sleep on Troopdeck E3, but many of us decided rather than sweat it out in that hole down in the ship, we would take our bedding up to an open deck for fresher air.

Sanitary and washing facilities were as bad as expected with eight wash basins for 500 - 600 men. These were hopelessly inadequate and, assuming one gained access to a basin, the taps were often dry.

The rest of the journey I describe from diary entries:

11 August:

> *'Now well out at sea. Slept last night curled up on the foredeck. A strong wind was blowing and it was cold enough for one blanket. The sea has been rough today, due probably to monsoon conditions - large amounts of cumulonimbus and cumulus clouds'.*

The 'Franconia'. Before becoming a wartime troopship this cunard liner was on the New York - Liverpool Atlantic run.

12 August:

'Still quite rough due to swell and people are still being sick. By now I've got my sea legs and feel quite fit. So far I've taken all my meals, although most of the fellows have missed at least one meal.

From 12.00 hrs 11th to 12.00 today the ship covered 352 miles. There is much speculation on when we shall reach Aden.

The wind is howling and the foredeck is running with water due to spray. Tonight I shall sleep on the aft deck where it is dry. It is so hot on E3 troopdeck that I couldn't sleep there if I tried. The atmosphere is hot and unpleasant'.

13 August:

'Last night was colder than anything I've experienced for quite a while. A howling gale blew over the deck where I slept and in the middle of the night I was wearing two blankets.

The food is still fairly good, but isn't always quite adequate in quantity.

Still rough today, but most seem used to it. The ship still rocks from end to end, but the wind has dropped off slightly so we may be moving out of SW monsoon conditions.

A few chaps on the foredeck were nearly washed overboard last night and, as it was, had their bedclothes soaked with sea water.

Ship did only 338 miles from 12.00 yesterday to 12.00 today, probably due to heavy seas. Shall be glad to see land, this is a monotonous sort of existence.

Once at Aden the worst of the rough seas should be over for a while'.

14 August:

'Sea calmer now and no one is feeling ill, a bad thing in a way since everyone now attends meals and food is none too plentiful.

Mileage covered during past 24 hours - 329.

Sleeping down below, as the decks are out of bounds due to last night's little episode'.

(At midnight 14/15 August whilst we were at sea India and Pakistan achieved Independence. The appalling communal violence was tearing the old India apart. Imperial India was no more and although I did not know it, the 'Franconia' was the last troopship to leave India, so we were in a small way making an historic voyage).

15 August:

> *'Very calm day and at 12.00 we sighted Aden on the starboard bow. Couldn't see it clearly though, due to a mist. Later during the afternoon and evening we passed several mountainous pieces of land which could have been the mainland or islands.*
>
> *Quite a number of ships passed, all quite small freighters or tankers. Passed Barim Island this evening and from that point turned northwards.*
>
> *Slept below decks last night, but tonight I shall be on top again. Ship did 324 miles'.*

16 August:

> *'A really hot, sweltering day, and it's impossible to keep dry below decks, although up above it's little better. It's hard to keep clean, the washing facilities are so inadequate.*
>
> *Shall be glad to be home, this is boring and too uncomfortable to be enjoyable, although I am sure as a civilian passenger I would enjoy it.*
>
> *We are reaching Port Suez at 02.00 on the 19th and after that it should get cooler.*
>
> *Chocolate ration issued - six bars per person. Too much to eat at once (owing to the heat it soon melts).*
>
> *Passed an occasional ship and dolphins jumping in the water.*
>
> *Ship did 371 miles, the speediest'.*

17 August:

> *'Cooler day than yesterday owing to a strong wind from the north.*
>
> *Clocks put back one hour last night and even with an extra hour the day's run was only 363 miles'.*

'Very near land now, passed Brother Island this morning and Bhurdwan Island this afternoon and now in the evening land can be seen to port and starboard. Into Suez during the night.

Reading 'Talking of Jane Austen'. Did half an hour's fatigue at the meat store.

We have now completed almost half of the journey and ten days from now we should be home.

Slept on foredeck. Ship covered 352 miles.

The meat fatigue consisted of carrying around portions of animals -frozen solid and surprisingly heavy'.

The ship's tannoy used to let us know where we were and also how far we had sailed during the day. The islands mentioned I have yet to find on a map. From Bombay to Suez our average speed had been 14.3 nautical miles per hour i.e. 16.5 land miles per hour. No wonder air travel has virtually replaced sea travel for long distances.

'Woke this morning to find ourselves just off Suez and most of today has been taken in passing through the canal and this evening we are anchored at Port Said.

Passed two RAF stations and several army camps in the Canal Zone. The usual uncomplimentary remarks were passed between ship and shore.

Passed a number of ships in the canal including the Swedish 'Koell', the US 'William A Graham' and one or two more, including one from Oslo.

Several score of army chaps from Palestine came on board this evening. This of course makes the ship still more crowded.

The usual crowd of small boats in Port Said harbour selling leather goods. A crowd of chaps were throwing bottles at the boats. Had quite an argument about this. Some of the chaps on board this ship are worse than animals. Some of the Egyptian traders had goods stolen by our lot, items being passed to our ship with no money being sent back'.

(Goods were hoisted in the basket, removed, then passed

around, the poor Egyptian pleading for his money or return of handbags etc. This kind of theft sickened me and made me ashamed to be British)'.

20 August:

Woke up still in Port Said, but shortly after 06.00 we moved off passing by a crowded harbour full of ships including the 'Baltic', 'Reynolds', 'Wave Sovereign', 'Wave Regent', 'Arundel Castle' and the Swedish 'Monkfors'. There was also a ship from Helsingfors called 'Pansius'.

On fatigue this morning in the butchery hauling meat.

21 August:

Day in the Mediterranean completely out of sight of land. Ship's Concert this evening. Fairly good show.

22 August:

'Working in the hold this morning hauling meat up to 'B' Deck by means of a rope and pulley. My arms were quite sore by the time I had finished. I'm unused to strenuous physical work.

Met John Raby as I was finishing my morning fatigue and had quite a long conversation with him for the first time since 1944. Went over the usual religious ground, but I found my arguments were stronger than they were three years ago.

Passed Malta at 20.00, but apart from a flashing light saw nothing of the George Cross Island. I was disappointed in a way, since I had hoped to see it.

Sea is quite calm and we are making fair progress of 360 - 370 miles per day and are due in Liverpool a week from now'.

(John was now an officer. The officers usually slept in cabins once occupied by the passengers. We, the peasantry, were in the bowels of the ship. How we were physically able to meet each other is a long-forgotten mystery).

23 August:

'Woke to find Cape Bon off the port bow. Passed quite a number of islands and about midday saw Tunis and Bizerta. Also saw Los Angelo, the most northerly point in Africa. Bored to tears with this ship. There is so little to do of

interest. Cleaning out the hospital this morning - flooded with dirty water!

Food still inadequate, washing facilities hopeless'.

(Even my customary antidote to boredom, reading, was beginning to pall in those crowded conditions).

25 August:

'Passed Gibraltar at midday and had a perfect view of the Spanish coast and the Rock. Gibraltar rises shear from the sea and looks a formidable natural fortress honeycombed with caves and defences. I can see it's importance as a protection for the harbour area, but as a defence of the Western Mediterranean area it must surely be useless if an enemy holds the Spanish coast further west. This part of the coastline is just as high as Gibraltar, and could be quite as easily fortified and has the advantage of being nearer the Atlantic.

Later saw further parts of the Spanish coast.

Food still not too plentiful and I'm hopelessly fed up with this ship and some of the people on it. There is usually quite a bit of bickering about the food ration and various people accuse each other of having too much food'.

26 August:

'Quite cool down below during the night and early in the morning I had to put on a blanket.

Up on deck at 07.30 land could be seen to starboard - probably part of Portugal. Land was visible at 10.00 - again Portugal. Passed one or two small ships.

Sea fairly calm, but it is cool now and quite chilly on deck.

27 August:

'Day in the Bay of Biscay, but contrary to my own ideas of the Bay it was quite calm, due probably to an anti-cyclone over England'.

28 August:

'We are nearing the old country at last. This afternoon we saw a lighthouse off the Welsh coast and later in the day we arrived off the Mersey estuary. It was grand to see lights flashing from the misty coastline - the English coastline!

Officially we should disembark on Friday 29th, but now the date has been postponed to Saturday.

Wearing full blue now due to the low temperature.

Food now is appallingly inadequate and heaven knows I felt hungry while biscuits were on sale at the canteen; things were not too bad, but now it's impossible to buy anything at the canteen, supplies have run out'.

(Numerous packets of biscuits had kept me going, tiny little packets containing four or five biscuits. Once I was even reduced to taking slices of bread other people had left).

29 August:

'Woke up this morning, took a look through a port-hole and saw Liverpool.

Until 18.00 we anchored in the middle of the Mersey, near to the Liver building and the entrance to the Mersey Tunnel. Camel Laird's ship-repairing yards were quite near.

Watching the coastline all day - real English industrial scene, plenty of smoke and little fresh air.

The ferry boats have been plying back and forth all day between Liverpool and Birkenhead. Saw the 'Royal Daffodil' in which we crossed to New Brighton in 1939 when we stayed at Wavertree. Most of the passengers were clearly visible and it was good to see waving English civilians.

When we docked at 18.00 a crowd of civilians soon came along the landing stage to look for sons, husbands and sweethearts. Crowd of redcaps there - they were booed!'

Not only were the military policemen booed, but sadly some disembarking Indian civilians had verbal abuse hurled at them which epitomised the feelings some British servicemen had towards Indians. Once again I was ashamed of some of my fellow-countrymen.

30 August:

'Stevedores unloading tin boxes from the hold last night so we had no sleep and anyway had to be up at 03.30. Had breakfast at 05.30 and disembarked at 08.15 and passed through the customs officials (who were lenient) and finally were taken away in gharries to Burtonwood, Lancashire.

*At Burtonwood we were rushed through stores, had a meal,
filled in forms and were ready to leave at 17.00. Really it
was amazingly good organisation by the RAF. I will say
they did their best for us and the only real hold-up was at
stores.'*

Before leaving Burtonwood the met. assistants were told to go on leave,
then report back for a draft to Germany. There were no more than seven of
us and all except one were really annoyed. All of us had expected a UK
posting and the one exception who welcomed the posting to Germany was
me. To me it seemed a grand opportunity, though it was a bit tough to be told
you were to leave England again when you had only been ashore five hours.
The fact though was that Germany counted as a home posting.

That evening I took a train to Euston, crossing by taxi to Liverpool Street
which had an 02.45 train leaving for Norwich. Although it was summer I was
so cold that I snuggled into my greatcoat. My travelling companion was an
ex-POW who spoke well of his German captors. He said they had been
treated quite decently providing they behaved themselves. His viewpoint
would have been different had he been a Pole or a Russian. Thousands of
Russian POWs died in captivity.

There was a long wait at Norwich Thorpe Station, inhospitable in the
early hours of the morning, though preferable to the badly-bombed City
Station from which the earliest train did not leave until 10.00. In those days
the city was deserted in the small hours of the morning and I was conscious
of the sound of my own footsteps, the chiming of the many church clocks and
the smell of the breweries, all now closed.

The train took me as far as Holt where it terminated, no Sunday trains
being allowed to go as far as Melton Constable, it being the Sabbath. Leaving
my two kitbags at the station I set off on the near five miles journey home. I
was ecstatic as Belle View tower, a local landmark, came into view. Then
came the wonderful homecoming with my parents and brother. Raymond had
been eleven when I left for India, now at fourteen he had almost reached my
height. I had missed a chunk of his life, but it was soon as if I had never been
away.

After two almost sleepless nights I was exhausted and slept for thirteen
hours. India was in the past and soon, in a few months, the RAF would be off
my back.

CHAPTER 49

Disembarkation Leave; Return to Norfolk Roots

My disembarkation leave consisted of 28 days - one whole month to do as I pleased in a temperate climate with no orders to be obeyed and, above all, that wonderful countryside of north Norfolk. My cycle came out of hibernation and I travelled miles exploring an area of Norfolk where I had lived only a few weeks before being called up. The greenness was overwhelming after India and I experienced a wonderful, heady sense of freedom which I savoured to full measure. Churches were seldom locked in 1947 and I visited many, sometimes with my brother, sometimes alone.

Some miles away at Hempton was a German POW camp. I made several visits talking to prisoners through the wire mesh fencing. They could understand my German, but I understood them with less ease. Two in particular I liked and knew quite well. It seemed so unfair that they were still POWs two-and-a-quarter years after VE Day. I said farewell to one of them on 26 September and we corresponded briefly.

My German, such as it was, was practised on the Ukrainians too. These men had been in the German Army for many reasons. Many Ukrainians had been anti-Soviet and had the Germans not been so heavy-handed when occupying the Ukraine they would have had potential allies.

Three rail trips were made to Norwich, then a battered-looking city with much evidence of wartime air attacks. The City Station, long since closed, had temporary buildings and looked forlorn. The site of the present-day Debenhams was a vast water storage point in the basements of bombed buildings. The shops were so dull, rationing was still on and goods of every kind in short supply. Britain had a siege economy, the country was exhausted and Norwich looked it.

Fortunately the Cathedral and Castle had survived. On one of my visits to the latter I palled up with a German POW of the same age as myself. We had met at the Market Place and looked round the Castle where everything was 'Wunderbar'. How could I regard him as an enemy? It seemed so patently absurd. Once I left the RAF I would be a reservist with the possibility of recall. If we went to war again I faced a moral dilemma - to fight or refuse.

An organisation called German Educational Reconstruction had in their possession 3,000 Germans hoping to make contact with Britons. They had comparatively few British takers so to further the cause of internationalism and reconciliation I ended up with eight correspondents, five men and three women, some of whom I would have met once my German posting took place.

After the wartime break Football League fixtures resumed in Season 1946-47. This I missed, but was now able to resume watching professional football. During my leave I managed to watch Norwich City play two matches, losing 5-1 on each occasion. For the second successive season they finished bottom of the old Division 3 (South).

Like all good things the leave had to come to an end and as the day grew nearer my spirits sagged; I fell into my demoralising habit of counting off the days.

CHAPTER 50

Back to Burtonwood

My leave officially ended at 24.00 on Sunday, 28 September but since we had no Sunday trains I decided to go absent without leave for 23.59 hrs. reckoning I had a good excuse. So at 07.00 on the Monday, none too happy at the prospect of a return to the RAF, I set off.

The journey via London and Crewe took fifteen hours, the latter part of the journey in the company of a sergeant-pilot - one who <u>had</u> survived. Arriving at Warrington at 22.00 we caught a lorry to Burtonwood, located 3 miles north-west of Warrington. Burtonwood was a vast place and had been a USAAF base for four years. As well as an airfield it had also been an aircraft depot having no less than 44 hangar workshops and stores with half a million square feet of storage and a million square feet of workshops employing almost 20,000 men.

After going through the usual preliminaries, no one noticing my delayed arrival, I was directed to No. 1 Wing, but not needed I was sent to No. 2 Wing, at midnight at last finding myself a Nissen hut. I bedded down in the company of a crowd of RAF Regiment 18 year-olds. They were packing their kit and polishing all their brass, the lights finally going off at 02.30. Good, I thought - sleep at last! But not for long. At 04.00 some of them were up and dressed ready for a BAFO (British Air Forces Overseas) posting to Germany.

At breakfast I was pleased to see the familiar faces of met. lads from the 'Franconia' and moved into their billet only to be told on parade that we were to change huts. At afternoon parade the seven of us were informed that our 14 October posting to Germany had been cancelled and our names were off the draft list. Evidently the Met. Office wanted us in Germany, but the RAF who had the final say, thought it wasteful to send us so near demob. Their decision changed my whole life.

Thwarted of the posting to Germany, to which I had really looked forward, my hope now was a home posting to an aerodrome in Norfolk. Some had been closed, but there was still a good chance, so I applied accordingly.

In spite of it being still only October our Nissen huts, each containing twelve beds, were unbelievably cold. Burtonwood being further north than Norfolk seemed so much colder. To sleep in comfort I needed five thin blankets with my coat on top.

I was officially now in No. 1 Wing Pool Flight and spent part of one day in the XOS (ex-overseas) office, but next day it was cookhouse duty slicing bread with a machine. But when 'volunteers for a bit of writing' were called for I offered my services and resumed XOS work. Here we did clerical work, mostly airmen's postings. Our 'working' day was laughable and almost unbelievable. We began at 09.00, having a NAAFI break from 10.00 - 11.00 after which we slogged away for one whole hour. The dinner break was 12.00 - 14.00, duties concluded at 16.00. It was ridiculous, but ours was not to reason why.

Not being technically in transit we took meals with the permanent staff and had quite decent food. If insufficient, there was always the NAAFI for a 'top up' - a substantial fish and chip meal for one shilling (5p).

Five hundred airmen arrived from Japan, more mouths to feed, and I was again caught for cookhouse duty, cutting the eyes out of potatoes. Once I was on fire picket at No. 1 Wing Guardroom, but in general did XOS work.

Twice I managed a brief week-end break at home, happy to be with my own family and sleeping in my own bed. The journeys back were tedious. Crewe Station was a bleak place to spend three or four hours in the middle of a cold, foggy night. The waiting-room had a fireplace, but no coal. Men in uniform were everywhere, soldiers, sailors and airmen wandering the platforms or sitting huddled in the cold waiting-room with heads tucked in greatcoat collars. Once back at Burtonwood I managed about two hours sleep, but it was worth it. The weekend pass for such a long journey could have done with a few extra hours. I did suggest it to a senior NCO, but I was told 'This is the RAF not a _____ friendly society'.

I was now in another billet and what a queer bunch. Four had served sentences whilst in the RAF, and two were later dishonourably discharged. Another poor lad was a little on the simple side. Some years later he hit the headlines of the newspapers. He had stayed in the RAF and was involved in an offence concerning, of all things, an atomic bomb threat.

Demobilisation was going along nicely, but I still had a few months to go with one more hurdle, my next posting. On 15 October I was delighted to learn that I had been posted to West Raynham, an aerodrome only fifteen miles from home. The same day I left the vast depot of Burtonwood heading once again for Norfolk.

CHAPTER 51
Last Lap at West Raynham

RAF West Raynham was my final RAF posting. On Saturday, 18 October 1947 I caught a train to East Rudham railway station. With kitbag over shoulder I set off for the aerodrome's Guardroom, then trekked around with my arrival chit.

The Met. Section had no duties for me and suggested I might as well take the week-end off. In case anyone had second thoughts I was off like a shot, retracing my steps to the railway station, where a really attractive booking clerk sold me a ticket. She was about to come off duty. Having made sure I was in the same compartment we travelled together as far as Melton Constable. As it turned out the young lady lived in a village three miles from my home. The journey was momentous and affected my whole future.

Two days later I reported back, but searched the large barrack blocks in vain to find a bed. So I opted for a less permanent building on the Massingham Road site some 500 yards from the main camp. It was a bleak, cold, dull-looking, inhospitable hut with inmates less than sociable.

The Met. Office personnel, almost all civilians, were a pleasant crowd and the duties were not too arduous. As well as day duties (08.00 - 17.00) we had the occasional morning only, or evening only, duty. Successive night duties came round every few days. The trouble with these was the sleeping problem. Inconsiderate types would put the radio on full blast. Then there would be hut-repairing sessions by workmen. If time permitted I went home by train, cycle or hitch-hiking occasionally - anything for a decent undisturbed sleep by day.

Sometimes the aerodrome personnel who did not do essential shift work had what was known as a 'long weekend' pass from Friday to Tuesday. All flying stopped and the aerodrome was almost deserted. I enjoyed those breaks, though not eligible. For me it meant an empty billet and uninterrupted sleep.

16 November was a highlight day. Two of us managed to find a hut on our own, quiet and free of teenagers and their noisy habits. It was good while it lasted, but on 12 December we were winkled out and put in another large hut with all the attendant problems.

Our met. assistants included two likeable lads, both civilians, called Kiddy and Kelly, which sounded like a comedy act or a solicitor partnership. In the Met. Office the communication system by modern standards would seem primitive. Apart from the telephone we relied heavily on our two teleprinters. One night on solo duty, at 03.00, having been busily occupied, I neglected to watch the teleprinter. Whilst my eyes were off it, the machine was spewing out chewed up paper. Panic stations ensued, but by the use of the spare machine and the telephone I had everything in order when my relief arrived at 08.00.

That night someone deliberately tampered with our cloud searchlight. It was used to estimate the height of the base of low cloud and was operated by a switch in the office. Though reported to the Guardroom the culprit was not caught.

Machines were never my strong point, but even I plumbed the depths of stupidity when one night I phoned for a civilian to repair a teleprinter. The poor man travelled several miles, only to find I had inadvertently switched it off. The shame of it. I hope he was on double time.

Soon after arriving at Raynham I had called at the section that dealt with demobilisation enquires. Yes, they assured me, my turn would come by mid-December. But by early December I had heard nothing, although my demob-medical had been completed and my blue release book filled in. It was now apparent that unless the authorities got a move on I would not be released in December. Anyway the Demob Centre at Warton, Lancs closed down on 19 December for the Christmas break. Why the hold-up? The reality was that the documents, necessary for my release, had been sent from Burtonwood to Germany.

What of aeroplanes? Well, unlike Vizag in it's latter days, we did have flying. West Raynham under Air Commodore Harvey, was the home of Central Fighter Establishment which, to the RAF, was an air fighting academy. There must have been various types of aircraft there, but my mind is a blank and I recorded little. I do remember naval personnel. They belonged to the Naval Air Fighting Development Unit and took the title 787

Squadron. By this time my interest in military aeroplanes had waned. I just wanted to be out.

I did record on 25 November a Squadron Leader Lucas, in a Meteor twin-engined jet, attempting to beat the world's air speed record, but just missed it. He did with ease break the Edinburgh-London speed record.

RAF discipline irked me more than ever. The very first day I was in the billet minding my own business awaiting for my 17.00 hrs duty. In burst two bumptious NCOs demanding to know my reason for being in the billet during the day. Presumably they had never heard of RAF shift work. For such people I could hardly conceal my utter contempt, but it paid not to argue too much.

Argue I did with one squadron leader. The occasion was caused by missing pay parade whilst on duty. So armed with a chit from one of our forecasters I turned up for a casual pay parade, but was refused. This led to an argument when I was shouted down after standing my ground. I was accused of cheek, insubordination and other misdemeanors. The officer threatened to put me on a charge. We parted on the worst of terms - me without my money! Later, when a civilian, I read that this gentleman had been found guilty of embezzlement, cashiered from the service and imprisoned. My 'crime' in comparison seemed insignificant.

Some days later the SWO's Sergeant deemed me in need of a haircut and invited me to present myself to his superior's office, suitably shorn by 13.30 the next day. I duly complied, but dropped myself in the mire later in the day when, feeling hungry, I walked a little early into the Airmen's Mess for tea. Station Police were hidden inside and took down the numbers, names and ranks of those of who were a few minutes early. We heard no more of this wicked offence, akin in a way to Oliver Twist asking for more. It all sounds petty, but that is how it was. As my friend Iain once wrote:

'Follies committed in the name of service'.

The day, however, was not without it's rewards. For the second time I met that pleasant young lady from East Rudham Station, travelled together and chatted on arrival at Melton. In the words of 'Blind Date' the chemistry was right. Things were looking promising.

I again applied for the One Year Emergency Course for Teachers. The application was too late. Many ex-servicemen were thinking of a career in teaching. I applied for a two year course at St Paul's College Cheltenham, but there was no place available for September 1948, but did gain admission a year later when I was 23.

What a gulf separates 1947 from today. Wages were low, but so were prices. It was possible to buy a complete Linguaphone Course in German for £5, which I did. West Raynham decided on a 5 November firework display. This consisted only of a few Verey lights fired into the air. My diary also records collecting five week's sweet ration coupons. These entitled me to eight 2 oz bars of chocolate and 4 oz of sweets. Two-and-a-half years after the war and sweets were still rationed. Britons had virtually a complete decade of privation. As for cars, washing machines, telephones etc. these were beyond the aspirations of most of the population.

One day at home I cycled to the deserted ex-RAF aerodrome at Matlaske. What strange places when empty, poignant with a sense of history and atmosphere of eerie ghostliness. No aeroplanes, no airmen, the Control Tower open to all. Documents were strewn around for the taking. In retrospect I should have preserved them for posterity, but decided to leave well alone. No doubt they were ultimately thrown away.

21 December I fondly imagined would be my last ever RAF duty, confident that in the New Year I would be released. So off I went for ten days leave. It was so enjoyable to spend my first Christmas at home since 1943. One day after Christmas I enjoyed a glorious cycle ride to the coast; a wonderful sense of freedom visiting places such as Blakeney and Wiveton. Passing through the village of Sharrington I hoped to see a certain young lady, but was unlucky, there was no 'accidental' meeting.

On 2 January back at Raynham I called at the Release Section, but to my amazement found no word of my demob. I was furious and just left the aerodrome, with my anger directed against the RAF. I walked four miles, 'hitched' two lifts, ending up in Swaffham at my grandmother's house, where my mother and brother were staying. Next morning I managed another lift as far as the deserted Great Massingham aerodrome, walking along the main runway to nearby West Raynham.

My release date had now been fixed for 25 January, so for the time being it was back on the Met. Office duty roster. With the support of the Release Section personnel an attempt was made to bring the date forward, but the centre at Warton would have none of it.

There was now a temporary sleeping problem. The billet in mid-winter was now incredibly damp added to which, in my absence, someone had stolen my mattress. So it was off to the Met. Office to sleep until able to sort out where to put my head down.

Back on duty I did my best, but was resentful at being there at all. On one night duty I was only needed for ten minutes or so on the hour to do an observation. I tried sleeping between 'obs' using an alarm clock to wake me. The effect was unpleasant. I could see how sleep deprivation was used as a means of torture in the USSR.

Once again the cloud searchlight was put out of action. Some idiot threw a bucket of water over it. Yes, even in the RAF we had vandalism.

My final duty was from 08.00 - 17.00 on the 18 January which left a few days to 'clear'. I recorded mixed feelings, utter relief, yet fear of the unknown. There was an awful feeling that we were heading for World War Three and that my release might be only temporary. In fact, within five months the Russians would be attempting to starve out the West Berliners. The massive American-British Air Lift prevented this from happening, but the Cold War had begun in earnest.

At 16.00 hrs on 23 January, in possession of my precious documents and rail travel warrant, I cycled out of the main gate at RAF West Raynham - next seen in 1999.

Next day, having spent the night at home, I was up early and on my way to the railway station. On the train was Jean the young lady for whom, in spite of having seen her on only a handful of occasions, I had a growing attachment. I had earlier asked if she would go out with me, but our off-duty periods never once coincided. Before reaching East Rudham Station Jean gave me hope that we would be seeing a great deal of each other in the future. After she left the train I wrote her a letter which I posted at Peterborough.

Arriving at Lytham St Annes I made the journey to Warton my final RAF camp. Warton, like Burtonwood, had been a USAAF base with storage and repair facilities, but on a smaller scale. At Warton we were issued with sheets, allocated billets and handed in those all-important documents.

Next day, a Sunday, I walked to Lytham along the coast road then took a bus to Blackpool which, with everything closed, looked a cheerless place. A cold wind was blowing. After lunch in a small restaurant I walked along the beach, almost deserted save for a group of boys playing football. Stopping to watch I little realised the part schoolboy football would play in my future life.

On 26 January we were up early and by 08.00 had had an FFI (the last!), handed in sheets and were taken by lorry to the buildings at Kirkham where the demob process took place, the so-called 'demob machine'. They were fantastic. In one hour we streamed through an endless succession of rooms where forms were given out and items of kit handed in, including such mundane objects as knife, fork and spoon. Finally, the clothing section where we each selected a sports jacket, pair of trousers, raincoat, shoes, cloth cap and so forth. Our uniforms we were allowed to keep.

CHAPTER 52

Return to Civvy Street and a VIP in My Life

The journey home was memorable for it's slowness. The RAF had done an efficient job in swiftly 'processing' us at Kirkham and by 12.15 I was at the local station bound for Preston where a change was made for Crewe. Here it would have been easier to take a train to London, but the RAF rail warrant only gave the right to travel across country. So from Crewe it was on to Rugby, thence to Northampton, changing for Peterborough (change No. 5). A two hour wait until 23.00 at Peterborough when I was on the Norwich train (changing at Ely). Arrived at Norwich at 02.30, a long wait before walking across the deserted city to the long-vanished City Station. Catching the 06.30 train I arrived home nineteen hours after starting a journey of just over 200 miles - just one rail journey typical of wartime and early post-war Britain. But, at least then, most places were within a few miles of a railway station.

At journey's end I met Jean. My letter had been successful and that afternoon I was introduced to her parents. Later we cycled to the cinema at Holt. The film, 'Black Narcissus' may have been good, but I was far more interested in my companion.

My diary recorded:

'Feel in higher spirits than for many a long day'.

It was all happening.

Although no longer a serving member of the RAF in an active sense, my effective date of release (i.e. last day of service) was not until 19 April 1948. The intervening weeks were demobilisation leave. Even during those few weeks I had already made two vital decisions that affected the course of my life. I knew who my future wife would be and my career was settled.

Jean and I had developed a deep fondness for each other and by the end of 1948 were engaged. The following year we married.

The career? Well I approached Norfolk Education Committee and they sent me as a temporary, unqualified supply teacher to a small village school, Itteringham, where on 12 April (still in the RAF) I commenced my teaching career. Whilst awaiting teacher training at St Paul's College, Cheltenham I also did supply teaching at Brinton and Briston. All three schools closed many years ago, regrettably in some ways for the villages concerned.

Although I had looked forward to demobilisation it was not so easy to be a civilian again as I had assumed it would be. It felt odd not to be in uniform. In a uniform one wore the clothes of a much respected organisation, it hid one's identity. In civilian clothes I felt exposed. For most of my demob leave I wore uniform and not the civilian clothes with which I had been issued.

On one occasion in Norwich I wore my red demob pullover with my RAF uniform which led to an encounter with RAF police who, finding me improperly dressed, wanted my ID card, already handed in. Then I explained who I was, demobbed etc. Once, as two SPs approached, I provocatively thrush both hands in pockets and inevitably was stopped. All rather childish behaviour, but as this is a warts and all description of how I felt I have included it. I suppose it would be called SP baiting.

I was delighted to have found my lovely girlfriend and a profession I enjoyed as much as meteorology. Teaching was my niche, though I made many errors. Yes, 1948 was a wonderful year, but there was a cloud hanging over me, namely the threat of World War Three. Once the USSR started the Berlin Blockade things worsened.

At this time I was an RAF reservist. My Service and Release Book stated:

> *'Although released you have NOT BEEN DISCHARGED'.*

I even had a travel warrant for my return to a remobilisation station carrying the code letter 'S'. In a national emergency the location of 'S' would have been revealed in the press and on the radio. I remained a

Jean, the one good thing to come from my West Raynham posting!

221

'G' reservist until 1959 i.e. for eleven years. This was unknown until I read my RAF records this year!

What if I had been recalled? I had half made up my mind to refuse, my feelings at that time being pacifist. I wrestled with this problem and weighed it deeply, but fortunately was spared the decision.

With teaching and family occupying my time my attempts at Anglo-German reconciliation via letter-writing came to an end. Eventually contact was lost with Guptan, Bhattacharya and another Indian, Chatterji. As for the British airmen I had known at Vizagapatam 'Jock' Elliot and Iain Malcolm as I have said are no longer with us. Of the others I know nothing.

My loathing of the RAF in the latter months of my service mellowed with the passage of time. But it took many years before I came to terms with it all. My one and only medal was not claimed until 1977. But now looking back I have no regrets at having experienced RAF life in both war and peace. It was valuable to have met such a variety of people and to have lived in another country. My RAF service was my university.

It was a different world in the forties, no better or worse overall than the end of the century. It is a period of history now long gone and remembered by a dwindling minority of my countrymen. I am pleased to have been just a microscopic part of it.

The RAF motto is *'Per Ardua ad Astra'* - *'through hardship to the stars'*. I experienced something of the hardship, but was too much of a coward to reach for the stars at many thousands of feet. Had I done so this might well not have been written and some of my family readers might not exist!